MAGIC and WITCHCRAFT

MAGIC
and
WITCHCRAFT
An Illustrated History

Ruth Clydesdale

SIRIUS

For Philip Clarke (1944–2021)
magical companion, enchanted times

SIRIUS

This edition published in 2022 by Sirius Publishing, a division of
Arcturus Publishing Limited,
26/27 Bickels Yard, 151–153 Bermondsey Street,
London SE1 3HA

ISBN: 978-1-3988-2077-7
AD007999UK

Printed in China

Contents

Introduction

ON THE EDGE OF A DARK FOREST stands a tumble-down cottage. A bent old lady huddles over the hearth fire inside, stirring herbs into a cauldron as she mutters spells. By her feet sits a black cat, watching her actions with an uncanny appearance of intelligence. A besom leans against the wall next to a dark cloak and pointed hat.

Such is the fairy-tale vision of the witch – but did such a person ever exist? Throughout history, some old and eccentric women certainly knew herbal remedies and simple magical charms, but the historical record shows that people accused of witchcraft could be male or female, young or old, impoverished or in positions of power and wealth. Not even the clergy were immune to accusation. And today the witch is more likely to be your colleague, your friend or your neighbour. Witchcraft itself has changed its nature entirely over the past 100 years or so, reinventing itself as a religion that honours old Pagan gods, celebrates the ever-changing seasons of the year and, unlike most religions, revels in the sensuous pleasures life offers. Most witches today follow a strong moral code that forbids them to cause harm of any kind.

And what of magicians, standing robed and commanding in their mystic circle, conjuring demons to do their bidding? Here the archetype is much closer to the truth, and since late mediaeval times there have been such seekers who attempted to wrest knowledge and power from supernatural sources. But, like the witch, the present-day magician is a different creature; he or she may work with forces embodied in figures from popular culture, or roam the streets chalking up sigils to protect the environment.

Although these archetypal figures are more elusive than the stereotypes suggest, there is no doubt that both good and bad magic do exist, and have done since prehistory. It is speculated that prehistoric cave paintings of animals represent hunting magic, with the images conjuring up a good kill. The oldest animal representation so far found is in South Sulawesi, Indonesia, and shows human figures hunting pigs. It is estimated to be almost 44,000 years old. And all cultures show evidence of simple magical practices, such as the use of amulets and charms.

Despite the best efforts of rationalists and scientists, such beliefs have never died out; they

The popular fairy-tale image of a witch stirring her cauldron.

appear to be hard-wired into the human psyche. Magic is a way of attempting to exert some kind of control over an unpredictable and often dangerous world. Whether it works is another question entirely, and one that is beyond the scope of this book, in which we trace the history of witchcraft in the UK, Europe and America. We will look at the kinds of magic that people have variously utilized and feared, and at who used – and uses – magic. What we can say with confidence is that magic has a psychological effect, and to that extent it works. The Italian mother who hangs a phallic-shaped charm round her baby's neck feels that she is protecting her child against illness and misfortune, and she will feel better for doing so. Such practices are ancient, some change over time,

Red wild deer and hand stencils of prehistoric cave painting at Sumpang Bita Cave, Pangkep, South Sulawesi. The surrounding karst mountain range contains many cave paintings and rock art. The uranium dating results in the studied caves generally vary from 17,000 to 39,900 years old. The oldest is almost 44,000 years old.

and others stay remarkably consistent. However, the range of magic that is in use today is meagre compared to the feast of charms and techniques that were available to, for example, the Anglo Saxon tribes.

Much of magic has historically focused on protection. Travel charms, rituals to ensure a flourishing crop and a good harvest, protective spells for livestock; the last of these probably died out only during the 20th century. Ordinary people would pass down such knowledge, whereas for health problems, love magic and finding lost goods or treasure there were specialists known in the UK as 'cunning folk' available in most villages and towns.

If a person or an animal fell sick, or the crops failed, or a child died, natural causes were not always blamed. Any apparent failure of protective magic implied that someone was working against it with malicious magic that was more powerful than the beneficent kind. Thus arose the figure of the witch, greatly gifted with uncanny abilities but so warped in mind and emotion that he or she derived pleasure from using power (and profit) to harm others.

A different, far more elaborate, kind of magic was developed and performed by learned people (historically, almost always men) with far more ambitious aims: to meet one's guardian angel, command demons and gain universal knowledge. Along with such knowledge came the ability to command love, wealth and power.

Fear of the witch, together with more mundane motivations such as neighbourly disputes, led to one of the most appalling episodes in European history: the witch trials. We will look at those in due course, but they are far from being the whole story of witchcraft. The witch can also be seductive, supernatural, political or downright amusing. That is partly why the figure of the witch continues to unsettle and fascinate us. And an excellent way to understand the witch is to look at how the history of witchcraft unfolds. Witchcraft is a story that shows no sign of ending; indeed, it continues to refresh itself with extraordinary vigour. The same can be said of magic, as new schools are developed, and swiftly gain adherents through digital communication around the world.

The study of witchcraft and magic takes us into the world of imagination, away from the mundane round of daily life. Objectively, we can say that Satanic witches never existed; magicians in their protective circles may be contacting their own deep unconscious forces, and claims of ancient ancestry claimed by the main branches of Wicca (as contemporary witchcraft is called) cannot be proved and are, to say the least, extremely unlikely to be true. But the world of the imagination has its own reality and benefits, not least being the nourishing of a deep sense of wonder and awe that is invaluable in a jaded society. Let us now enter the world of magic and witchcraft.

Chapter One

Charms, Curses and Witches in the Ancient World

Bohemian peasants
believed that if they
fenced the entrance
to their stables with
thorns, this would
discourage witches
from entering and
working their wicked
spells on cattle.

Everyday Magic

THE SCENE IS SET IN EGYPT, during the 1st century CE. Freshly bathed and wearing a clean robe, a man turns towards the sun and takes a few steps forward. The only clue that he is performing a magical rite can be seen on his head, where a cat's tail is precariously balanced. He stops, and on the ground marks out a circle with mystical characters around it.

The man steps into the circle and recites a string of nonsense words. These are *nomina barbara*, secret names of gods endowed with great magical power. Looking directly at the sun (a foolish thing to do), he sees on its face a shadow. He shuts his eyes and looks away. When he opens them again, the shadow is standing right in front of him. Now he recites one more secret name and, the simple rite completed, commands the shadow to answer a question or perform a task.

The man might be a magician or just an ordinary person who had been instructed how to carry out the rite by a priest at one of the temples. At this period in history, Egypt was part of the Roman Empire (1st–4th century CE) and a melting pot for many races and religions. In such a climate, magic flourished. Many papyri containing spells, incantations and herbal cures, written in Greek, give vivid evidence of the popularity and range of magical practices. Some rites are lengthy and complex, requiring long periods of abstinence from sensual pleasures and certain foods before they can be carried out. Others are simple love spells, directions for making an amulet ring, or charms to cure illness. Many could, with a little

judicious adaptation, be used by witches and magicians today.

Take for example a spell for picking a plant. This very simple procedure must be carried out just before sunrise and consists of reciting a few sentences telling the plant why it is being plucked, and asking for its cooperation. Any magical practitioner today would adopt a similar ritualized approach, and there is much else in the papyri that is instantly recognizable. Magical practices conform to the culture of their time and place, but the basic nature of many of them appears to be eternal, reflecting the unchanging needs and wishes of the human heart.

We tend to think of ancient Greece and Rome as being the sites where rationality developed. That is correct as far as it goes, but it is far from being the whole picture. Throughout the course

Magical practices conform to the culture of their time and place, but the basic nature of many of them appears to be eternal...

An Egyptian magician is initiated into his calling: he is subjected to sensual temptations which he must resist.

of ancient history, the use of magic was an integral part of people's lives right across Europe and beyond. A whole variety of techniques was available, from those mentioned above to curses and binding spells. Physical evidence of cursing still exists, since curses would be scratched into thin sheets of lead and then either buried or cast into water. Many of these have been recovered from the Roman baths at Bath and other sites.

A disturbing example of binding magic can be seen in the Louvre museum in Paris. The artefact comes from Egypt in the 2nd century CE; it is pot containing a clay image of a naked woman with a Roman hairstyle. She is kneeling, with her hands apparently bound behind her back, and she has been pierced by 13 needles in her eyes, breasts, genitals and elsewhere. Someone either hated this woman enough to want to make her life intolerable, or lusted after her and wished to make her suffer until she gave in to his desires. Whatever the reason, the effigy is vivid proof that ancient peoples did not pull their punches.

Spells for working malevolent magic tend to attract more attention than positive magic simply because they are so dramatic and shocking. However, analysis of ancient magical techniques has proved that more methods existed for working helpful magic than for doing harm. The latter are largely confined to binding and cursing, although cursing can have a wide range of objects from jinxing a rival's team in a chariot race to causing crops to fail. Good magic was used to increase confidence, make the practitioner lovable, cure a variety of ailments, gain a supernatural servant, ask questions of the gods, gain promotion or the favour of a powerful patron and so on. Amulets were worn for general protection against dark forces and for good luck. Magic could be applied

Voodoo doll on exhibit at the Louvre museum. Bound and pierced with thirteen pins, it was found in a terracotta vase with a lead tablet bearing a binding spell.

Ankh talisman, also known as the "crux ansata", is the ancient Egyptian emblem of life.

to each and every situation in life, and both men and women performed it or frequented sorcerers to work on their behalf.

Some very simple magical folk remedies for pain must have been passed between people orally. The Roman writer Varro (116–27 BCE) records a healing charm for foot pain. The simple formula must be repeated 27 times when sober:

> I think of you; heal my feet; let the earth retain the illness; let health remain here, in my feet.

– Georg Luck, translator, Arcana Mundi

A plethora of similar healing charms exist in the Greek magical papyri and other literary sources, most of which also emphasize the need for sobriety – which gives the unexpected impression that drunkenness was rife in the Graeco-Roman world.

Healing illness or setting broken bones ranked high amongst the many ways in which ordinary people used magic. On occasion, herbs are recommended, and it's possible that using magic and herbal remedies was safer than consulting a professional. This is a theme that continues through time and various cultures until the rise of scientific thinking in Europe during the 17th century. However, even then doctors in the UK continued advertising unicorn horn as an effective remedy against plague and other assorted ills, a practice that died out only in the first half of the 18th century.

War, food shortages and illness made life precarious, so ways of predicting the future were highly valued. A number of public oracles became famous in the ancient world, such as the Pythian oracle at Delphi, and much more humble methods

The Pythian oracle at Delphi reveals mysteries and predicts the future while in a state of entrancement.

for do-it-yourself oracles were also common. The Greek magical papyri describe several rituals of varying complexity for obtaining an answer in a dream. One method of receiving a "yes" or "no" answer simply requires the practitioner to light a lamp at bedtime and recite, in multiples of seven, an incantation including a couple of *nomina barbara* with a request for a dream of a plant and water for "yes", or iron and a fire for "no". Whether or not the practitioner was visited by such a dream, the act of concentrating on the question might have been enough to clarify the desired answer and suggest an appropriate course of action.

A rich variety of other methods of divination could be employed. Any unusual phenomenon, anything that catches the attention, could be seen as an omen. A significantly timed sneeze, an overheard phrase, a door swinging open or an object falling could all be fraught with meaning. The weather and the behaviour of birds and animals were also read; in effect, the world and everything in it was woven into a vast and complex pattern of meaning in which human lives were included.

Artificial divination methods ranged from those needing no skill (such as picking at random a phrase from Homer) to ones requiring learned knowledge, such as elemental divination using earth, water, air or fire. For instance, an air oracle could be obtained by throwing a handful of earth, sand or seeds into the wind and then reading the pattern made when the grains landed.

Although all such techniques would have been used as needed, there were also recommended times for performing particular magic acts. The zodiacal position of the moon was crucial, so a basic table of lunar positions would be needed.

In effect, the world and everything in it was woven into a vast and complex pattern of meaning, in which human lives were included.

When the moon was in Leo, for example, the consecration of magic rings was favoured, as were binding spells. An Aquarian moon aided love charms, and when it reached Pisces divination fell under the spotlight.

Another subject of profound interest was the gaining of good luck and protection, along with the banishing of bad luck. Anyone who had been suffering a run of bad luck could perform a simple scapegoating spell. All they had to do was choose a small and inessential item into which to cast the bad luck. Then it was enough to light a lamp and, holding the item, pray to Hecate that one's ill fortune be bound to the item so that it harmed no one. The item would then be buried or burned.

An engraving by an unnamed artist of the worship of Isis at a festival in ancient Egypt. Worshippers could bring items to be charged with protective power in a ritual setting.

Protective spells tended to be addressed to one of the gods, such as Isis, and to be fairly complicated. Personal items such as rings could be charged with protective power in a ritual using incense, libations of milk or wine, and lengthy prayers.

Once thoroughly protected from harmful influences, the practitioner would be well set up for working some helpful magic. Love spells could, as we have seen, be coercive and vengeful towards the recipient, but gentler spells were also available. A simple one required the lover to obtain a picture or statuette of the love goddess Aphrodite, and to burn incense to it while repeating her secret name Nepherieri. The next time the beloved was sighted, the lover was to repeat the secret name over and over while gazing upon their intended, and to repeat this for seven days. If the prolonged staring and muttering didn't put off the beloved, he or she may just have felt flattered by such intense attention.

Businessmen and women enjoyed access to a range of spells to draw the favour of Hermes, the god of trade (and of sharp dealing). These are based on placing a statuette of Hermes in the business place and doing it honour with offerings and libations.

A handful of charms deal with social situations still relevant today. Hermes could also be invoked for help with a poor memory or other mental issues such as clarity of speech or preparation for examinations. Shy people could ensure popularity by the simple means of repeating a phrase from Homer under the breath: "Let no one sleep, lest we become a joy to our enemies." Whilst the phrase has no relevance to the problem, the mere act of repeating it secretly could perhaps rouse up courage to face demanding social situations.

A 19th-century wood engraving of Hermes (lat. Mercurius), known as the messenger of the gods, that is based on a classical ancient statue.

One's own or another's anger could be controlled by silent repetition of another phrase from *The Iliad:* "Will you dare raise your mighty spear against Zeus?"

The magical papyri also contain a fair proportion of spells and charms that from the modern point of view were highly unlikely to work, such as becoming invisible by sleeping with a snapdragon flower under the tongue and then reciting a string of *nomina barbara*. A bold magician who obtained a skull might use it for divination – but the papyri warn that such speaking skulls might not only be useless at their task, but even worse – they might never shut up.

One final example: a cure for shyness. Before a social occasion, the shy person's face was to be smeared with gum mixed with wine and honey. Surely this must have been a cruel joke?

Goddesses of Witchcraft and Magic

The Greek magical papyri give vivid glimpses into a multicultural society in which magic was deeply embedded. To see what beliefs underpinned such practices, it's necessary to look far back into Greek myth and legend.

So absolute was the ancient Greek belief in witchcraft that it had its own goddess, Hekate. One account of her origins states that she was one of the Daughters of Night, and night was certainly her time. She was thought to spend the nights roving around at the head of a band of ghosts, accompanied by the sound of barking dogs. Anyone waking from sleep in a state of panic was said to have been attacked by Hekate. She was also known as the mistress of the Underworld, which associates her with the more familiar goddess Persephone, the unwilling bride of Hades, the king of the dead. The myth of Persephone's capture and removal into the Underworld recounts that Hekate went with Persephone's mother Demeter to ask Helios, the sun god, if he had seen where the young goddess had been taken.

Hekate is a great goddess, whom Zeus himself revered and to whom he gave a share of three realms: the sky, the sea and the earth. Her own form is triple, as she is associated with the moon that can be seen as passing through three phases every month: waxing, full and waning. Statues of her were erected at places where three ways met; these had three faces positioned so that each looked along a path. Such crossroads were places of ill repute where convicts were buried so as not to pollute the places where people lived.

Hekate is a complex goddess, but one thing is clear: she is associated closely with women. As such, she was one of the goddesses to whom a woman in labour would pray. Sometimes she helped the process, but she could also hinder it. As the goddess of witchcraft, she gave her divine blessing to women who worked sorcery.

Hekate's salient characteristics entered into European witchcraft beliefs and are still with us today. The Great Goddess of Wicca, the modern-day witchcraft, is triple in form, and sometimes invoked as Hekate. She is still the goddess of the moon, along with the Roman goddess Diana. Covens often meet after dark, although not at

✝ *Ancient Roman marble statue depicting the triple-faced goddess Hecate or Hekatea.*

crossroads – and not accompanied by ghosts and barking dogs.

But what did witches get up to in the ancient world? The Greek poet Homer gives us the earliest description of a woman working magic. He probably composed his two epic poems, *The Iliad* and *The Odyssey,* around the end of the 8th century or beginning of the 7th century BCE. In *The Odyssey,* the tale of Odysseus' interminable journey home after the Trojan War, Homer includes a description of the hero's encounter with the beautiful sorceress Circe.

Circe is not human but a goddess; one account makes her the daughter of Hekate. Her speciality is turning men into animals or birds; when king Picus resisted her advances, she transformed him into a woodpecker. When Odysseus' ship lands at her island, Circe appears to welcome his crew. She feasts them, but puts a drug in the food that makes them forget their homeland; then she strikes them with a magic wand, turning them into pigs. Homer leaves her reason unstated, but it is possible that she is merely revealing their true nature. Here we can see how ancient the idea of the magic wand is.

When Odysseus sets off to find out why his crew hasn't returned, he meets Hermes, also a magically inclined god, who carries a golden wand as well as his famous snake-entwined caduceus. Hermes gives Odysseus a herb called Moly, which acts as an antidote to Circe's drug. Her magic overcome by that of Hermes, Circe becomes helpful and friendly. After a year during which Odysseus enjoys every kind of pleasure with her, she returns his crew to human form and sends them on their way. But first, she instructs Odysseus in a necromantic technique for receiving wise counsel from the long-dead blind prophet Tiresias.

The goddess of magic Circe, who was the daughter of Helios, god of the sun, and – in one account – Hecate.

Illustration by C.E. Brock showing Circe the sorceress turning Odysseus' men into swine.

The word used to describe Circe's witchcraft is *pharmakon,* which has a range of meanings from cure to poison to magic. The word pharmacy derives from it. This linking of medicine with magic – both good and bad – indicates that the origin of medicine lies in magical practice, and it is a thread that can be followed through until the beginning of modern medicine.

The story of Circe is clear-cut, but it is a very different case with the other famous witch from myth, Medea. She first enters mythology as a woman with no special powers, a princess who falls in love with the adventurer Jason and helps him steal the Golden Fleece from her own father. However, according to later accounts, Medea was a niece of Circe, and her grandfather was Helios, the sun. That lineage turned her, like Circe, into a goddess. Her tale was told in many ways and she developed into the archetypal image of a malevolent witch.

The epic poet Apollonius of Rhodes (fl. 3rd century BCE) wrote a chilling description of Medea casting the evil eye on Talus, a bronze giant who tried to destroy Jason's ship, the *Argo,* by hurling rocks at it. Medea invokes the Hounds of Hades three times, filling herself with their lethal power before casting the evil eye at Talus. The giant duly grazes his ankle, which is his sole vulnerable point; ichor (the gods' equivalent of blood) runs out of the hole and he dies. Even though Medea is helping Jason and his crew, she is depicted as a terrifying witch.

The most familiar retelling of her story is Euripedes' play *Medea,* in which she and Jason are married for ten years and she performs much helpful magic on his behalf. But then Jason abandons her to marry the King of Corinth's daughter, prompting a terrible revenge. Medea

is another worker of *pharmakon,* and she uses her malevolent knowledge to poison the wedding gifts she offers to the princess and her father. Not content with dealing them a horrible death, she completes her revenge on Jason by murdering the sons they'd had together. After this terrible deed she flees in a chariot drawn by dragons; it is said that passing over Thessaly, she throws overboard all her remaining herbs and potions. Eventually she makes a good marriage to King Aegeus, one of the mythical founders of Athens. What happens after that is variously told, but Medea's worst days of wicked magic are over.

Circe and Medea together establish the archetype of the seductive but evil sorceress. Their tales mirror each other. Circe begins by working malevolent magic before turning helpful; Medea starts by helping Jason until his treachery drives her to malevolence. From these early tales is derived the view of female witches as being dangerous, even though they perform both good and evil magic.

Literary Witches

So far we have seen the goddess witches using a magic wand and herbal potions for their magic. What more can literary sources tell us about how magic was done in the ancient world?

Literature was largely but not exclusively a male pursuit in ancient Greece and Rome. The accounts of magic that have survived are by men, which could account for the predominance of sorceresses and the somewhat sensational view of them. Women were regarded in both cultures as inferior in every way, and that derogatory view fed into ideas about the magic they might be practising.

First, though, we look at a rather sympathetic vision of a witch. The Sicilian poet Theocritus (c.300–270 BCE) wrote a lengthy and beautiful lyric about Simaitha, a young girl who falls head over heels in love with a local athlete, Delphis. Not knowing how to attract him, she seeks help from many old witches, but their spells are to no avail. Eventually she sends her maid Thestylis to meet Delphis and tell him that Simaitha longs to see him. Delphis duly turns up in her bedroom, where she lies sick with longing. Apparently with practised ease, he takes command of the situation, blandly telling Simaitha that he had been on the point of visiting her anyway, and assuring her of his love.

Thus does the naïve young Simaitha lose her virginity. Delphis enjoys her embraces every night until, 12

days later, another girl catches his eye. A gossipy neighbour informs Simaitha of his new love, and in desperation she decides to work magic herself and recover her unfaithful lover by a complex binding spell.

Simaitha winds crimson or purple strands of wool around a cauldron over a fire. Then she casts in a variety of items, using sympathetic magic to make the erring Delphis burn with agony. Barley grains, laurel, wax (possibly shaped to look like Delphis) and a piece of fringe from Delphis' mantle all go into the fire as Simaitha pours libations. Then she gives her servant magic herbs to smear on the lintel of Delphis' front door. All the while, Simaitha is revolving an iynx, a magic wheel to draw Delphis to her house. The iynx was a hand-held metal wheel, toothed around the edge. A loop of cord was passed through two holes at the centre and wound tight. When unwound, the wheel made an eerie whistling sound. Originally a wryneck bird

The Sicilian poet Theocritus, who lived circa 300–270 BCE.

Painting showing Queen Anne as Britannia, with Christian Truth and a prophetess. The Sibyl-like figure, or prophetess, on the Queen's left, holds an open book. The inscription is a quotation from Lucan's "Pharsalia" or "Civil War" and means, loosely translated, that no-one goes to war for the sake of rights or in defence of laws, but only in pursuit of glory and gold. The Queen's Drawing Room *by Antonio Verrio (1636–707).*

Sextus Pompeius consulting Erichtho before the Battle of Pharsalia (oil on canvas) by John Hamilton Mortimer (1741–79).

This region of Greece enjoyed an unparalleled reputation for witchcraft for reasons that are little understood. It may be that Thessaly was sufficiently remote for Romans to fantasize about it as a barbaric place given over to evil practices.

(*iynx* in Greek) was attached to the wheel. This magical implement was widely known and in popular use for well over a millennium.

Theocritus clearly knew his magical techniques well, as every detail of Simaitha's ritual can be checked in the Greek magical papyri and other sources. Theocritus lived in Alexandria for a while and may have picked up a lot of magical information there. We are not told, however, whether the magic worked. Two hundred years later, Virgil was so charmed with Simaitha that he wrote another version of Theocritus' poem, this time supplying it with a happy ending in which the girl's lover returns to her.

Poor naïve Simaitha is a sympathetic character, but not so the three witches depicted by Horace (65–8 BCE). The main protagonist, Canidia, plaits vipers into her hair; her nails are uncut, her teeth yellow. She and her two companions ritually torture and murder a boy in order to cut out his liver to use in a love potion. They bury the boy up to his neck and torment him by placing food just out of his reach until he dies in agony. Such repugnant cruelty obviously exists only in Horace's imagination, in contrast to Simaitha's spells. The difference surely lies in a perceived gulf between a woman who uses magic – as many ordinary people did – and an actual witch, imagined as a woman who uses magic to do nothing but harm.

So begins the enduring caricature of the witch as an ugly, evil old woman. Another Roman author, Ovid (c. 43 BCE-18 CE), adds the qualities of a bawd, a woman who pimps girls to men. First Ovid establishes the image of his character Dipsas as a witch who can work weather magic, use poison and practise necromancy. But none of these powers are relevant to her attempted persuasion of a girl to give herself to a rich lover; it seems Ovid describes them merely to establish the wickedness of her nature.

Once established, there is no escape from this caricature. Perhaps the nastiest depiction of a witch is Erichtho, which may have originated with Ovid. She appears in several literary works, most famously in Lucan's (39-65 CE) *Pharsalia*. In this unfinished epic poem about the civil war between Caesar and Pompey, the latter's son asks Erichtho to reveal which side will win the impending battle of Pharsalus.

Lucan sets the scene with a lengthy fantasy about witchcraft in Thessaly, where the scene is set. This region of Greece enjoyed an unparalleled reputation for witchcraft for reasons that are little understood. It may be that Thessaly was sufficiently remote for Romans to fantasize about it as a barbaric place given over to evil practices. The mythical reason that its witches were so

Perhaps the nastiest depiction of a witch is Erichtho, which may have originated with Ovid.

numerous and skilled lay in the tale mentioned above: when Medea escaped from Corinth in her dragon-drawn chariot, she threw away her magic materials over Thessaly.

Thessalian witches were thought to be uniquely powerful; it was said that they could draw down the moon, which probably meant that they could cause an eclipse so that the moon seemed to have been pulled from the sky. Lucan lets his imagination run riot; he claims that all the Thessalians are impious and horrible people, and the very ground supports a plethora of poisonous herbs. Thessalian witches are able to compel the gods of other religions to do their will; they can slow down time, halt rivers and terrify lions and tigers. They excel in the use of poisons, but Erichtho – the worst of them – scorns all such activities as too lightweight. Her speciality is working with the dead, although she also blasts crops by breathing upon them. She is, of course, ancient and loathsome to look upon. Erichtho buries the living and reanimates the dead. She even feasts on corpses and, whenever she needs fresh blood for a ritual, she commits murder or tears an unborn child from the womb. Lucan's descriptions are extremely gruesome; for instance, here is Georg Luck's translation from the *Arcana Mundi* describing Erichtho stealing a criminal's corpse:

With her teeth she bites through the fatal noose on the rope and plucks the corpse dangling from the gallows; she scrapes criminals off the cross, tearing away the rain-beaten flesh and the bones baked in the glaring sun. She takes off the nails that pierce the hands, the black juices of corruption that drip all over the corpse, and the clotted fluids, and when a tendon resists her bite, she pulls it down with her weight.

In answer to Pompey's son, Erichtho performs a gruesome ritual to reanimate a corpse from a battlefield, and compels it to give a prophecy, which turns out to be rather ambiguous. Obviously no good comes of consulting such an evil witch.

Philosophers or Magicians?

The figure of the ancient Greek philosopher presents quite a vivid contrast to the literary witch. These men, we have been led to believe, were the first in Europe to experiment with the logical, rational mode of thought that sowed the seeds for the development of science. However, many philosophers were complex people who also enjoyed reputations as powerful sorcerers. The ones we know about are all men. There was a significant handful of women who defied convention and became philosophers, but little is known about them with the exception of Hypatia (c.360–415 CE), a Neoplatonist mathematician and astronomer whose fame mostly rests upon her terrible death at the hands of a Christian mob in Alexandria. Since the Neoplatonists were known to practise magic, and since mathematics was considered a magical art and astronomy was at that period tightly entwined with astrology, Hypatia may well have been seen as a sorceress.

Delving back into the early days of Greek philosophy takes us deep into the realms of magic. Pythagoras (c.570–495 BCE) is credited with inventing the word philosophy, or "love of

 A sketch of Empedocles (c.495–435 BCE).

wisdom"; he is thus the very first philosopher. Legend records that the Thracian priest Abaris gave Pythagoras a golden arrow on which he flew; one of his thighs was also golden. He could bi-locate and was simultaneously seen in Metapontum and Croton. The natural world acknowledged him; the river Kosas was heard to greet him as he crossed it.

Another famous pre-Socratic philosopher was Empedocles (c.495–435 BCE), a well-to-do Sicilian. Empedocles' words survive only in quotations by later writers, so there are doubts about their accuracy. All the same, some who knew Empedocles claimed that they had witnessed him working magic, and in one quoted passage from Jonathan Barnes's translation in *Early Greek Philosophy*, he promises to teach one of his pupils some distinctly un-philosophical skills.

*What drugs there are for ills and what help
against old age
you will learn, since for you alone I shall
accomplish all this.
you will stop the power of the tireless winds
which sweep over the earth
and destroy the crops with their breath,
and again, if you wish, you will bring on
compensating breezes.
And after a black rain you will produce a
seasonable drought
for men, and after the summer drought you
will produce
tree-nurturing streams which live in the ether.
And you will lead from Hades the power of
dead men.*

Here is Empedocles making an ascending series of promises, as if setting out a course on magic. He starts off with what might be taken as an offer to teach medicine, but is more likely to imply the magical use of herbs; passing on to weather magic, he culminates triumphantly with a claim that his pupil will be able to raise the dead. That unsavoury feat was also, of course, performed in loathsome style by the witch Erichtho.

Let us move forward in time now to the great Neoplatonist Plotinus (c.204–270 CE), who lived in Roman Egypt at the time the Egyptian magical papyri were being compiled. Plotinus was fortunate in having a devoted pupil, Porphyry (c.234–305 CE), who put his rather chaotic writings in order and also wrote his biography. In the latter, Porphyry says that Plotinus suffered a magical attack from Olympius, a philosopher who was envious of his success. The vicious magic caused Plotinus dreadful cramps, but he threw the spells back at Olympius so that the wicked philosopher /

sorcerer found his limbs convulsed and his whole body "like a money-bag pulled tight" – a description found in Stephen MacKenna's translation in the book *Plotinus: The Enneads*.

Magic was fundamental to Plotinus' philosophy. Plotinus describes in detail the principle of *sympatheia* (sympathy or affinity), a technical term used by the Stoics. This universal principle of attraction is the basis of magic. Plotinus states that magic is a natural phenomenon obeying cosmic law, and it holds the universe in bonds of harmony: "There is much drawing and spell-binding

Plotinus, Greek philosopher (c.204–270 CE): Roman sculpture from the 3rd century.

dependent on no interfering machination…true magic is internal to the All." Another name for *sympatheia* is Love, which Empedocles had declared one of the two defining forces of the universe, the other being Strife.

For Plotinus, magic is a natural force that not only holds the cosmos together but also dominates the life of the ordinary person. He understands how little we mortals are in control of our lives and how helplessly we wander hither and thither in pursuit of our desires. We fall under a spell every time we long for something attractive. Anything can exert a magical lure, be it a person, an object or an idea. Extracts from MacKenna's translation show the philosopher's view of the matter:

> *[E]verything that looks to another is under spell to that: what we look to draws us magically…Hence every action has magic as its source and the entire life of the practical man is a bewitchment: we move to that only which has wrought a fascination on us.*

The English word "fascination" derives from the Latin verb *fascinare*, meaning to bewitch. The state of being bewitched implies an inability to think or act independently, because the bewitcher is in control. Every time a desire arises, the soul gives up its freedom.

While the ordinary person lives in a state of almost constant enchantment by the world, he can also employ human magic. The magician caters for those who are in thrall to their desires, helping them attain their ends. And to do this, he learns to utilize and enhance the natural cosmic magic in much the same way that a gardener will use his skills to manipulate nature. A good magician knows how to employ the patterns of *sympatheia*

in the natural world. Metaphorically, he can lay his hand on the right rope to reel in the desired object: "He pulls knowing the pull of everything towards any other thing in the living system."

Learning magic is a process of understanding which natural substances, rites and circumstances will bring about the desired result. For example, a spell for a successful business might involve carving a statue of Hermes and offering it frankincense and coins at a time when the planet Mercury is powerful, as in the Greek magical papyri. Plotinus states that once the magician has learnt the correct clusters of sympathetic substances and invocations, he can, for example, "work love magic as simply as training two trees to knit together".

Unfortunately, he can also fling curses in the way that Olympias did. However, the universe being an orderly and harmonious place, misusing magic brings unavoidable results:

> *A man may…help himself to what lies open to all, but if he does so beyond what is right, punishment follows by ineluctable law… The punishments of wrongdoing are like the treatment of diseased parts of the body…and the penalties are planned to bring health to the All…*

Here Plotinus puts Olympius' sorcery in context, implying that he himself acted as instrument of the cosmic law by causing Olympius to suffer the results of his evil action.

The philosopher's intense concentration on the spiritual life has implications for the efficacy of magic. The accomplished philosopher, whom Plotinus calls a Proficient or Sage, can to some extent remain immune from magic because he no longer feels desire for anything in the material

world. When the Sage is meditating on the spiritual world, he can't be touched by magic: "No man self-gathered falls to a spell; for he is one, and unity is all that he perceives." Being intent on the divine core of his being, the Sage has withdrawn from the material world; hence, magic cannot work on him.

Other Neoplatonists such as Iamblichus (c.245–325 CE) also both employed and wrote extensively about magic. Iamblichus' treatise *On the Mysteries (De Mysteriis)* is virtually a handbook of magical techniques that relate very closely to the magical papyri. According to his biographer, Eunapius, Iamblichus came from Chalcis in Syria, and was descended from the priest-kings of Emesa. After studying with the saintly Christian Anatolius of Laodicia, Iamblichus turned to Neoplatonism and studied with Porphyry in Italy. He returned to Syria in about 304 CE and founded his own school in Apamea. Iamblichus appears to have gone right to the roots of philosophy and rebuilt it from there as a system of practice as well as intellectual learning. He integrated magical processes

Iamblichus (c.245–325 CE) was a Syrian Neoplatonist philosopher and magician.

In order to invoke the presence and power of the solar deity, the philosopher/sorcerer has to bring together as many of such related items as possible, although at moments of dire need a single item may be employed. This principle of sympathetic planetary magic is still used in magic.

and traditional religious forms of worship with Neoplatonic philosophy and meditation techniques.

Iamblichus' pupils seem to have been as keen as anyone on some supernatural excitement. One time, they got into such an argument over whether Iamblichus had magical powers that they begged him for irrefutable proof. Reluctantly, Iamblichus agreed. At a bathing place named Gadara, where there were two springs, he spoke quiet words over the water and conjured up the spirits of the springs, two beautiful boys who treated him with affection and respect. The springs were called Eros and Anteros – Love and Answering Love.

It fell to the last great Neoplatonist, Proclus (412–485 CE), to boil down the magical technique of sympathy introduced by Plotinus in his brief but hugely influential treatise *On the Sacred Art (De Sacrificio)*. Proclus explains that 'All things are full of gods,' and gives the example of the lotus opening and turning to the sun as an example of sympathy between the two. Also linked to the sun by sympathy are animals such as the lion, with its flaming golden mane, and plants such as the palm tree, with its rayed-out leaves. In order to invoke the presence and power of the solar deity, the philosopher/sorcerer has to bring together as many of such related items as possible, although at moments of dire need a single item may be employed. This principle of sympathetic planetary magic is still used in magic.

Magic on Trial

The philosopher/sorcerers seem to have practised their magic in peace, perhaps because they did so circumspectly. Others were less fortunate, and records of trials in ancient Greece and the Roman Empire show that prosecutions

The Twelve Tables, Rome's first legal code, are drawn up by a commission at the request of the plebeians.

for working magic were far from unknown. The trials cover a vast time period, from the 4th century BCE in Athens to the end of the 4th century CE in the Roman Empire.

The Romans passed a whole series of laws against magic, starting in 451-450 BCE with the Twelve Tables, which forbade anyone from magically transferring his neighbour's crops into his own fields. Astrologers were expelled from Rome in 139 BCE and again in 33 BCE, and from the whole of Italy three times in the 1st century CE. The emperor Constantine I, in the 4th century CE, issued a ruling that allowed helpful magic but outlawed destructive practices. Such frequent legislation demonstrates both how ubiquitous and how resilient magical practices were in Roman society.

In most cases, the accusation of magic hid a political motive or one of simple greed – in some cases both. Powerful political enemies could be destroyed and their property seized; a prime example is the case in 16 CE of Marcus Scribonius Libo Drusus, a distant relative of the Emperor Tiberius. Libo was a rich man who had a passing interest in occult arts, which gave ambitious junior senator Catus ammunition against him. When Libo made the mistake of consulting a man named Junius about necromancy, Junius reported him to another ambitious man, the prosecutor Lucius Fulcinius Trio. Libo was immediately charged with plotting against the Emperor and, realizing he was doomed, took the traditional Roman way out and committed suicide. His property was divided up between his accusers. Tiberius reacted by expelling all diviners from Rome – except his own.

The case of Tiberius' adopted son Germanicus was documented by the historian Tacitus (c.56–120 CE) and

is related in Georg Luck's translation of *Arcana Mundi*. Germanicus was a popular man, but he made enemies of the governor of Syria, Piso, and his wife Plancina. When Germanicus fell ill, he suspected that the couple had poisoned him, but his friends thought that magic was involved. After he died, these friends brought in workmen who found that whoever had wanted Germanicus dead had done a thorough job of cursing him:

> *Under the walls and between the walls of his house the remains of human bodies were found and dug up. There were also spells and curses and lead tablets with the name "Germanicus" engraved and, furthermore, half-burned ashes, smeared with blood and other tools of evil magic…*

The trial of Lucius Apuleius of Madaura (c.124–170 BCE) also had a financial motive; the difference is that Apuleius won his case – and he really does seem to have been knowledgeable about magic. Apuleius was born in a Roman colony in present-day Morocco; his father was a wealthy provincial magistrate whose death left his son very well off. Apuleius was able to study in Carthage, Athens and Rome, where he pursued a successful career in law. Later, he travelled widely in Asia Minor and Egypt. There were times when the hedonistic life he enjoyed brought him close to ruin, but he seems to have settled down after being initiated into the mystery cult of Isis. During his travels, Apuleius picked up a great deal of religious, philosophical and magical knowledge.

His main claim to fame is his entertaining novel, now known as *The Golden Ass,* a witty fantasy tale about another young man called Lucius, whose curiosity about magic ends with

The death of Germanicus, painted in 1627 by Nicolas Poussin (1594–1665), believed to have been either poisoned or dealt a blow by malevolent magic.

him being turned into an ass.

Right from the first page, the novel is shot through with magical tales – some amusing, others terrifying. Most are incidental to the plot, but they establish a sense that magical events are woven tightly into ordinary life. When Fotis, the maid of Lucius' host, tells him that her mistress practises magic and can shapeshift, Lucius insists that they spy on her. Such curiosity spells his downfall. He and Fotis watch as the woman smears herself with ointment, mutters a charm and turns into an owl. Foolishly, Lucius is seized with the desire to try the spell, and persuades Fotis to steal some of the ointment. Fotis knows the remedy, so the experiment appears quite safe. But Fotis steals the wrong ointment, turning the hapless Lucius into an ass.

The remedy is for him to eat roses, but a whole series of mishaps and adventures befall him before he is granted a vision of Isis, who instructs him to approach her High Priest during a procession and eat the roses he will be carrying. Lucius succeeds in doing so and, in gratitude, becomes a devotee of the goddess. Since Apuleius

The North African writer and philosopher Lucius Apuleius of Madaura.

himself became an initiate of Isis, the adventures of his namesake appear to have some autobiographical content, although it is difficult to say how much. Apuleius' own life was really quite adventurous enough to satisfy anyone.

While on his travels, Apuleius fell ill in Libya. Luckily, an acquaintance from Athens University days was on hand to take him in and nurse him back to health. Pontianus lived with his widowed mother, Pudentilla, with whom Apuleius soon became friendly. Pontianus confided in him that doctors had recommended that Pudentilla get married again for the good of her health, and he begged Apuleius to propose despite the ten-year difference in their ages. Apuleius did so, and Pudentilla made over her considerable fortune to him. But no good deed goes unpunished, and so it was that when Pontianus died soon afterwards, his relatives were quick to accuse Apuleius of poisoning his friend. However, they dropped the accusation when they decided a more damning charge would be that of winning Pudentilla's heart by enchantments.

The relatives had miscalculated. Being trained in law, Apuleius was ideally placed to conduct his own defence, and at his trial he delivered a scintillating speech in which he had a great deal of fun making his accusers look like absolute fools. His mercurial wit flashed across a number of unlikely topics, including tooth-whitening powder, his own unkempt hair, and a long disquisition on fish. Apuleius knew that *magus* is the Persian term for priest, and that philosophers such as Empedocles had worked magic; he said he was proud to be counted among such exalted company. He got the whole court on his side by making them laugh before proceeding to rebut in the most sober and eloquent terms the charges against him. He walked free; it is to be hoped that he and Pudentilla were allowed to live in peace henceforth.

Little did Apuleius know that his lighthearted novel and other writings would give rise to theories leading to the witch-craze in Europe. St. Augustine of Hippo (354–430 CE) developed a powerful hatred of Apuleius and devoted time and effort to criticizing his work, focusing particularly on Apuleius' theory of daemons (helpful spirits). Apuleius held the standard Neoplatonic view that daemons were of all kinds, including good ones that could be very helpful to humans. Augustine, however, categorized all such spirits as demons, that is, Satan's fallen angels (evil spirits). Such spirits existed solely to deceive humans. Anyone entering into a pact or understanding with a demon put their soul in danger by willingly

Little did Apuleius know that his lighthearted novel and other writings would give rise to the theories leading to the witch-craze in Europe.

surrendering themselves to the Devil. A thousand years later, this is the charge that would be levelled at men and women accused of witchcraft.

This overview of magic in the ancient world shows that, although the idea of enchantment evoked a great deal of doubt and fear, simple folk charms and remedies were an essential part of many people's lives. The alluring subject of magic provided material for myth and literature, but if used as an accusation it could end a person's life. Magic and witchcraft were real enough to have serious consequences; hence they were taken seriously.

Roses from the High Priest of Isis turns Lucius back into a human being.

Chapter Two

From Anglo-Saxon Elves to Magical Sacraments

Pagans and Christians

WE LEFT THE ROMANS regarding magic and witchcraft with fear and fascination. As the Roman Empire expanded across the Middle East, North Africa and Europe, soldiers were not only recruited along the way but also settled in various places. This meant that both soldiers and administrators came across a variety of new cultures. Those who travelled took their gods with them, and often recognized their own deities in disguise among other cultures. Thus the Empire brought about a great mingling of religious and magical beliefs and practices. The Greek magical papyri burst at the seams with invocations to Christian saints cheek by jowl with Greek and Egyptian deities, Jewish holy names and influences from Babylonian religion. As we have seen, witchcraft and magic were feared enough to be banned in Rome many times, but with only temporary effect. People at all levels of society continued to work their own charms and consult professional magicians as the need arose.

When the Roman Emperor Constantine the Great (c.272–337 CE) first showed leanings towards Christianity, magic was already understood as being best pursued with discretion. By 380 CE, Emperor Theodosius had decreed Christianity to be the official religion of the Empire. But where magic was concerned, the Church faced some problems. The 2nd-century Pagan philosopher Celsus had written a scathing attack on Christianity in which he pointed out that Christ's miracles were no different from the wonders worked by many contemporary sorcerers. The

Church was forced into the position of claiming that, whilst Christ's supernatural feats drew on God's power, those of other sorcerers such as Simon Magus derived from the Devil. By extension, then, all acts of magic except those performed under the auspices of the Church were evil – even such simple ones as pronouncing a charm over a wart. However, priests daily performed legitimate magic in the Mass, in which bread and wine were believed to be physically changed into the flesh and blood of Christ.

The Church was forced
into the position of
claiming that, whilst
Christ's supernatural feats
drew on God's power,
those of other sorcerers
derived from the Devil.

A magical contest between Simon Magus, representing magic, and the saints Peter and Paul: the saints won and Simon is said to have converted to Christianity.

Celtic Enchantments

Let us turn now to look at magic in Great Britain. Here, as across Europe, several kinds of magical practices had been part and parcel of life since prehistoric times. Observation of the sun, moon and other celestial bodies formed the basis of astrological practices; the spirits of place and human ancestors were honoured with deposits of artefacts and burials at significant places, and the magic of shapeshifting found expression in crafts decorated with fantastic animals. A striking example of shapeshifting between species is the Lion Man of the Hohlenstein-Stadel, found in a cave in Southern Germany in 1939. The figure has the head of a cave lion and a partly human body, and was carved in mammoth ivory, using flint tools, 40,000 years ago.

By the Mesolithic Age (c.10000–8000 BCE) we come across the ritual placing of objects in water across Europe and Scandinavia. This practice continued right up until the Iron Age (c.500–100 BCE) and probably well beyond. For example, when a man died, his weapons would be ceremonially bent, so as to be useless, and cast into running water. Not only weapons met such a fate; the Dover Bronze Age boat was deliberately sunk by cutting through the thongs that bound the planks together. The famous Battersea Shield may even have been crafted especially for a particularly grand sacrifice, since it is too small to have been of

The Lion Man of Hohlenstein, carved from mammoth ivory is the oldest sculpture in the world and is aged at about 40,000 years old.

The Battersea Shield was originally used for ceremonial purposes and was found in the River Thames in 1857. The horned bronze helmet (found near Waterloo) features similar red enamel bosses.

*A druid lunar
ceremony.*

practical use. Such mysterious practices find later echoes in mediaeval literature, as we will see.

Although we cannot say without doubt what such deposits meant, it is likely that they were given as gifts to the spirits of the land and water. Ancient people took from the land, just as we do, but they also felt an obligation to pay for what they had taken. Sacrificing useful and valued objects may well have been a way of fulfilling that obligation. The giving of a gift also laid a responsibility on the local spirits to give in return – perhaps in the form of a good harvest, healthy animals and abundant fish.

Water has an otherworldly quality for several reasons: humans can't breath in it; streams appear mysteriously from underground and can also vanish below the surface; water can evaporate into thin air and form again apparently out of nothing. Both running and standing water were probably seen as liminal places where the solid world of humans met the mysterious spiritual world. But the whole landscape of Britain was magical. Around the time that Stonehenge, with its famous solstitial alignments, went out of use, in about 1520 BCE, field systems began to be laid out that were also aligned to the solstices. Even though fields altered in size and shape over the centuries, the system of alignment was followed for the next 2,000 years.

Celtic culture spread across much of Europe as far west as Ireland from about 1200 BCE, and many traces remain today in folklore and myth. The wise men of that culture – the Druids – seem to have been advisors to royalty as well as priests, and their image has endured, attracting many tales along the way. However, it seems they indeed possessed powers to be respected and even feared – if a Druid hurled a sarcastic joke at

a warrior, it could be enough to kill him on the spot with embarrassment. Anne Ross, in *The Pagan Celts*, writes:

> *Other peoples agreed with its inhabitants that Britain was a highly magical place, with Pliny (23–79 CE) remarking that, "At the present day Britannia is still fascinated by magic, and performs its rites with so much ceremony that it almost seems as though it was she who had imparted the cult to the Persians."*

The passing of the year was marked by regular festivals, starting with Imbolc on 2nd February, associated with the goddess Brigid, who was adopted by Celtic Christianity as St. Brigid. Then followed the celebration of spring, Beltane, on 1st May. High summer and harvest were celebrated on 1st August, Lughnasa. Finally, on 31st October came Samhain, marking the start of the winter and the slaughter of stock for food during the long, cold months ahead. Modern Pagans still celebrate these festivals.

Fortunately, today's Pagans do not subscribe to one of the most prevalent and magically potent practices of Celtic cultures: the use of the severed head. In Celtic belief, personal and spiritual power was concentrated in the head, and any warrior who decapitated his enemy proudly displayed the head hanging at his belt or fixed on a lance point as he rode. Heads were also placed on hill fort ramparts or gateways as protection. Gold-decorated skulls were used as drinking cups.

In Welsh mythology, the tale of Bran the Blessed recounts how the wounded warrior Bran requests his followers to strike off his head. When they do so, the head remains alive and the company enjoy a life of feasting and merriment in

A beautiful image of St Brigid, whose origins are believed to be intertwined with the Celtic goddess Brigid.

an otherworldly place, until one of them breaks a taboo and they are ejected into the human world again. Bran's head is buried beneath the Tower of London, where it remains to protect Britain until King Arthur demands it be dug up, arrogantly claiming that he alone is sufficient protection for his country.

The Celts recognized many deities, including a god with stag's horns, Cernunnos, who has become one of modern Paganism's principle gods. There was another horned Celtic god as well, whose name has not survived; he had bull's horns. Both gods demonstrate the close kinship the Celts felt to their animal relatives.

Celtic goddesses were powerful figures associated with the fertility of the land and stock, and with battle. They tended to take a triple form, such as the raven war goddess The Morrigan. The

Cernunnos, horned deity of fertility and abdundance, was honoured by the Gauls and other Celtic peoples.

Painting by John Henry Frederick Bacon (1868–1914) showing the Irish hero Cu Chulainn meeting The Morrigan.

Roman sculpture of the Matres or mother-goddesses seated on a bench, wearing tunics and holding cups and possibly fruit, at the Housesteads Roman Fort Museum, Hadrian's Wall, Northumberland, England.

Celtic gods frequently entered the human world and had to be treated with respect. The gods lived magical lives, so their worshippers would appease them with charms, incantations and rituals. Magic infused every aspect of life as a way of negotiating with the supernatural powers that could both bless and curse human existence.

When the Roman army invaded Britain in 43 CE, they brought their gods and magical practices with them. Over time, these blended with native gods and magic. Thus in 725 CE, the Benedictine monk known as the Venerable Bede wrote of a Pagan custom celebrated on Christmas Eve and known as the Modranecht, or

✠ *A curse tablet found in Bath, showing a complaint about theft. This curse includes a list of names of possible culprits, including the name Vilbia, who may have been a slave.*

Night of the Mothers. This is thought to relate to a trio of goddesses known across northwestern Europe, of whom more than 1,000 statues have been found, dating from between the 1st and 5th century CE. Inscriptions give various titles to the goddesses, but they are generally known as the Matres or Matronae – that is, the Mothers or the Matrons. This triplicity of goddesses appears to be an example of Roman and European deities mingling. Thanks to the triple goddesses of Celtic culture, the image was powerful enough to travel and be accepted widely. What a crying shame that Bede either did not know or refused to reveal just what the annual rites of the Mothers were!

We might not expect
a wise goddess to be
adept at cursing people,
but evidently that was
a speciality of Sulis
Minerva.

Local deities were also Romanized. Perhaps the best-known example is that of Sulis Minerva, originally known simply as Sulis, the Celtic goddess of the hot spring at what is now Bath, in Somerset. The Romans perceived some similarities with their goddess of wisdom, Minerva, and blended the two. We might not expect a wise goddess to be adept at cursing people, but evidently that was a speciality of Sulis Minerva. About 130 lead tablets or *defixiones*, mostly bearing curses, have been recovered from the spring; they form the most important collection in Britain. Here we have another example of water being regarded as a portal into the world of the gods and spirits.

The Coming of Anglo-Saxon Magic

Following hot on the heels of Roman cultural influence in Europe came Christianity, which, as we have seen above, became the official religion of the Empire in the 4th century CE. Celtic Christianity was already known in Britain at this time, appearing to have reached Ireland in the early years of the 3rd century CE. In the Celtic land of Wales, it took its place among a mixture of Roman and local beliefs. Roman troops were withdrawn from Britain in stages, between roughly 383–410 CE, leaving the islands undefended against Anglo-Saxons from northern Germany and Scandinavia. These fierce warriors poured in, establishing kingdoms and bringing their northern gods and magic with them. The Celtic Christians do not seem to have attempted to convert these new invaders, but left them to their own beliefs. Thus Britain enjoyed an incredibly complex brew of Celtic, Roman, Christian and Saxon religious and magical practices.

The Anglo-Saxons' religion was founded on the concept of a triple world, linked by Yggdrasil, the world tree. Places of worship included both temples and natural sites such as sacred trees, hilltops and wells, where votive offerings would be left and animal sacrifices performed. Some places were sacred to a particular god, the most popular being Odin, Thor and Frig, whose names survive in place names such as Thundersley (Thor's Grove). Older Celtic influences mingled with the newcomers' beliefs; for example the spirit of the river Severn seems to be a Celtic undine or water spirit called Sabrina, from which the name Severn derives.

A variety of other supernatural creatures thronged the Anglo-Saxon landscape: elves, dwarves, giants, helpful household spirits, dragons and wodwose (wild, hairy, humanoid wood dwellers). All of these had to be dealt with, propitiated or avoided. Elves were particularly dangerous because they caused illness. The

The Scandinavian deity Odin (Wodan) acquired knowledge of the runes by hanging for nine days from the branches of the world tree Yggdrasil.

Sabrina, nymph of the River Severn, with her attendants.

Painting by Richard Doyle (1824–83) shows a moonlit landscape, with a witch herding young dragons, 1876.

Anglo-Saxon magic took
forms familiar to us by
now, employing herbs,
charms and wax or
dough figures – the latter
being used to either heal
or harm.

evidence for this lay all around in the shape of
flint arrowheads, which we know to have been
chipped by prehistoric people, but which Anglo-
Saxons interpreted as disease-bearing elf-shot,
fired from elvish bows at hapless humans. This
belief proved remarkably resilient, surviving in
Scotland until at least the 17th century, and in
Ireland until the early 20th century.

As in Celtic culture, the year was marked by
regular festivals, although there is a woeful lack of
written evidence about the form such celebrations
took. We do know, however, that in 700 CE
Theodore, Archbishop of Canterbury, imposed
penances on people who garbed themselves as
stags during a January festival.

Anglo-Saxon magic took forms familiar to us
by now, employing herbs, charms and wax or
dough figures – the latter being used to either
heal or harm. If harm was intended, the figure
would be stabbed with needles, burnt, hung up
or 'drowned'. Malicious weakening of a person
could be effected by reciting a charm, as related
in *A New History of Witchcraft* by Jeffrey B. Russell,
and Brooks Alexander:

> *May you be consumed as coal upon the hearth,*
> *May you shrink as dung upon the wall,*
> *and may you dry up as water in a pail.*
> *May you become as small as a linseed grain,*
> *and much smaller than the hipbone of an
> itchmite,*
> *and may you become so small that you become
> nothing.*

Many charms, both symbolic and practical, existed
for healing. Blood loss could be slowed and stopped
by reciting, "The maiden Hille has spoken / the flow
of blood is checked." A recipe for removing warts
simply advised mixing a dog's urine with a mouse's
blood and smearing it on the warts.

While ordinary people would have had
a whole repertoire of such simple charms at
their disposal for daily use, some used magic
(or the threat of it) to extort money from their
neighbours. A 6th-century law prescribed
whipping as punishment for storm-makers who
extracted protection money from farmers to
spare their fields. Sorcerers might also charge for
causing illness in a rival's family or animals, or
for making a man impotent.

Laurence, Archbishop of Canterbury, shows his lacerated body to King Eadbald of Kent. The wounds were the result of a vision in which St Peter whipped him in order to convince Laurence that he should make further efforts to convert Eadbald, a Pagan, to Christianity. (c.617 CE)

Magic continued to be practised while Christianity slowly spread across Europe, but curiously, until about 1300, there is very little sign of witchcraft as understood or imagined by the Christians. Indeed, the Church itself was rather deeply implicated in magic, as we shall shortly see.

The Christianization of Britain only really began around 600 CE, when Ethelbert, King of Kent, became the first English king to be baptized. Ethelbert had married a Frankish Christian princess, Bertha, and his conversion was a canny political move to cement powerful continental allies. Christianity at this time was very much the religion of the rich and powerful; most ordinary people carried on worshipping their old familiar gods.

When Ethelbert died, his son Eadbald became king and lost no time in reverting to Paganism. Archbishop Laurence of Canterbury was understandably disturbed by this, and eventually persuaded him back into the Christian fold. Eadbald may well have worshiped both Pagan and Christian divinities, since this practice was not unknown. King Redwald of East Anglia hedged his bets by maintaining both Pagan and Christian altars.

Early Christianity in England was a kind of exclusive club for those in power. The vast majority of Kentish Anglo-Saxons would have worshiped the northern gods: Odin, Thor, Freya and the rest. Unfortunately for us, the tradition was oral rather than written, so the only evidence of Pagan religion we have is from Christian sources (which are naturally biased) and what can be gleaned from folklore and customs.

Pagan religion seems to have been deeply rooted, so much so that the early Christians decided to adapt rather than destroy it. In a famous letter, Pope Gregory the Great wrote to Abbot Mellitus:

> *I have come to the conclusion that the temples of the idols in England should not on any account be destroyed. Augustine [the first archbishop of Canterbury] must smash the idols, but the temples themselves should be sprinkled with holy water, and altars set up in them in which relics are to be enclosed. For we ought to take advantage of well-built temples by purifying them from devil-worship and dedicating them to the service of the true God.'*

We also learn from this letter that these attractive temples were garlanded with flowers and had bowers constructed around them. Unfortunately they were wooden, as were the images inside them, so nothing has survived. The evidence suggests that such places of worship continued to be used into the so-called Christian era, as the 7th-century Penitential of Theodore attests:

> *If anyone sacrifices to demons, let him do penance for at least one year…If anyone shall have eaten or drunk at a Pagan shrine unknowingly, let him promise never to repeat the act, and do penance for 40 days on bread and water…*

Practical Magic and Its Sorcerers

The Anglo-Saxon magic that has come down to us is practical, focusing on such matters as curing illness in both humans and animals, ensuring good crops, finding stray cattle and gaining protection against the dangers of travel. The magic employs ritual and the recitation of charms in verse form. As well as protective and healing charms, some herb-craft has been recorded, and several means of divination. A variety of amulets has been found in graves, presumably placed there for magical or protective purposes. These can be made of gold, silver or quartz; there are also amber or jet beads inscribed with letters or words of power, and animal parts such as boar's teeth or eagle claws, together with fossils such as ammonites. Amulets made of herbs in a linen bag would also have been worn, but such materials have not survived.

The three main written sources for Anglo-Saxon magic and medicine are the *Lacnunga* manuscript, *Bald's Leechbook* and the *Old English Herbarium*. These manuscripts were copied out by monks during the 10th century, probably recording charms that had been in use for a long time. They give no clue as to who originally used them or under what circumstances, but they were probably for semi-professional men and women who worked in their own home locality. For the sake of convenience, we will call these people wise men and women; later they will be known as cunning folk.

Since the status of women was higher in Pagan Anglo-Saxon society than under Christianity,

they are just as likely to have been healers and magicians as men. In fact, Scandinavian literature contains plenty of evidence that women had acted as healers, diviners and shamanesses since ancient times. For instance, in the saga of Eric the Red, a female seer is consulted about a disastrous famine in Greenland. She eats a meal of animal hearts and sits in the centre of a circle of women to whom she teaches a chant that they repeat until she enters a trance and becomes possessed. The spirits then speak through her, giving assurance that the famine will soon end and going on to offer predictions for many of those present.

Many necklaces with amulets have been found in the graves of Anglo-Saxon women, as well as small crystal balls; small spoons with holes in them have also been found. It is thought that a well-to-do woman might have worn a crystal ball on her belt together with a spoon. Archaeologists have argued from this that some if not all women had particular magical skills that they did not share with men. It's speculated that the crystal ball would have been dipped into a magical or medicinal potion to purify it, while the holed spoon would have filtered out bits of herb.

Women were also perceived to fulfil the role of the witch by casting harmful spells. However, *Bald's Leechbook* supplied a simple remedy: 'Against a woman's spell, after fasting for a night eat the root of a radish; on that day the spell will not have power to harm you.'

Alfred the Great (c. 848-899 CE) took a far sterner view, anticipating the witch craze that would later cause havoc throughout Europe: 'The women who are accustomed to receive…spell-workers and mirage-dealers and witches – do not allow them to live.'

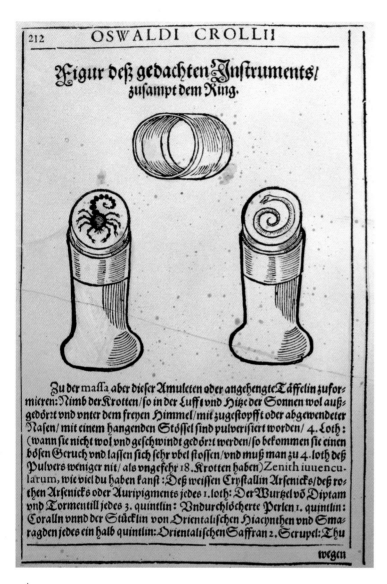

A woodcut of instructions for an amulet against poisoning from
Frankfurt, Germany, c.1623.

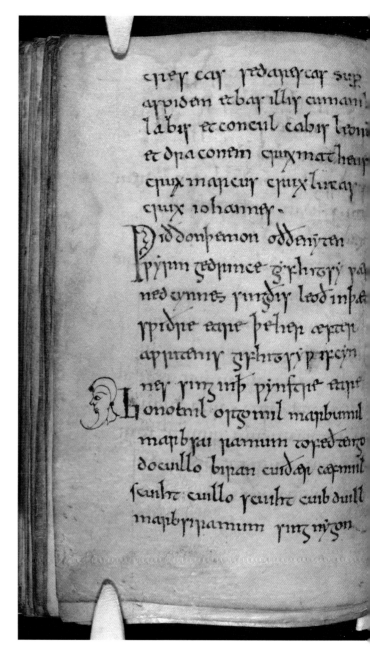

The Lacnunga, detailing charms that used writing
to gain their potency.

A card from the LeNormand oracle showing a man consulting a Wise Woman in ancient times.

Pagan Magic and a Christian Princess

While there were spells and divinations that anyone could practise, there were others that needed book learning, and some that required access to a priest and a church. Here's an example of a spell that anyone could do. It's for a woman who has difficulty bringing her unborn child to term.

> The woman who cannot rear her children easily should take the milk of a cow of one colour in her (cupped) hand and then sip it with her mouth and then…(go to) running water and spit out the milk into it and then with the same hand scoop up a mouthful of the water and swallow. Let her then say these words:
> *Everywhere I carried with me the wonderful …*
> *stomach-strength;*
> *… then I wish to have (success) for myself and*
> *return home (with it).*
> When she goes to the brook she should not look round, nor when she leaves, and then she should go into some other house than the one she came from and there take some food.

Now, it's possible that a woman may have to consult a wise-woman or man in order to learn this spell in the first place; on the other hand, it's simple enough to be passed down from mother to daughter. The same is likely to be true of the charm to stop a swarm of bees from escaping:

> Against bees (swarming): take earth, throw (it) with your right hand under your right foot and say:
>
> *I catch (it) under my foot, I have reclaimed it.*
> *Lo, earth avails over all creatures,*
> *and over malice and over jealousy*
> *and over the tongue [i.e. spell] of the powerful*
> *person.*
> *And from above cast the soil over (the bees)*
> *where they swarm, and say:*
> *Settle ye, war-women, sink to the ground! ?*
> *Never should you, wild, to the wood fly. ?*
> *Be ye as respectful of my welfare*
> *as is every man of food and shelter.*

As for divination, the casting of lots had been popular since ancient times, and in its simplest form could be practiced by anyone. Nowadays we still use the 'short straw' method, or toss a coin. There were also simple formulas for alphabet divination, dream interpretation by moon phase, weather prediction etc. But more serious questions might require the use of seers such as we've seen in the saga of Eric the Red.

Healing was effected not just by a charm but also with the use of herbs, and although most people would doubtless be aware of the basic uses of many herbs, we are moving here into the terrain of the wise-woman. Such is the Nine Herbs Charm, which lists the nine sacred herbs of the Anglo-Saxons and cures infections or diseases. The charm is lengthy; it invokes both Odin and Christ, and includes a verse to each of the nine herbs celebrating their power over illness. Here's a taste of it:

A worm came crawling (but) it destroyed no one
when Woden took nine twigs of glory,
(and) then struck the adder so that it flew into
nine (pieces).
…
Chervil and Fennel, very powerful pair:
Those herbs the wise Lord created,
holy in the heavens, when he was hanging;
He confirmed and sent (them) into the seven
worlds
for rich and poor, for all a remedy.
…
Christ stood over disease of any kind.
I alone know of a running stream
and there the nine adders keep guard.
May all plants now dwindle to their roots,
seas (and) all salt water disperse
when I blow this poison from you.

The wise-woman grinds the nine herbs, which
are mugwort, plantain, lamb's cress, cock's-spur
grass, camomile, nettle, crab-apple, chervil and
fennel. Then she mixes them with soap and apple
juice. This concoction seems to be combined with
a paste of fennel, beaten egg, water and ashes.
The spell has to be sung three times over each
herb before preparing them, and again before
applying the salve to the mouth, ears and skin of
the sufferer. Such a complex procedure probably
required a confident professional to perform it.

We don't know at what point Christ was
added to this or any other charm, but his presence
illustrates the way in which Pagan and Christian
practice intermingled without any problem.
Some charms indeed require the use of a church
and the participation of a priest. One such is
the Land Ceremonies Charm for ensuring good
crops and healthy livestock. This is a lengthy and

Legal codes prove that men of the cloth rather frequently got into trouble for offering magical services such as the Land Ceremonies Charm. Church law demanded the defrocking of clergy who allowed people into church for Pagan purposes. Clergy were also penalized more heavily than lay persons for consulting diviners or using talismans…

complicated procedure that includes a priest in church singing a mass over each of four pieces of turf, preceded and followed by the farmer reciting various Christian prayers and blessings over them. And yet the same charm implores the help of Erce, "Mother of Earth."

In fact, legal codes prove that men of the cloth rather frequently got into trouble for offering magical services such as the Land Ceremonies Charm. Church law demanded the defrocking of clergy who allowed people into church for Pagan purposes. Clergy were also penalized more heavily than lay persons for consulting diviners or using talismans, interpreting dreams or offering herbal healing: they had to do penance for five years as against a lay person's three years. That doesn't seem to have stopped them, however. For example, one herbal charm suggests that 'A mass priest shall perform the leechdom if a man hath means to get one.' This implies that the priest must have charged rather heavily for his services; indeed, the price of treating a sick cow with herbs and a recital of the Lord's Prayer was a tenth of the animal's value. The wise-man or woman probably charged less in the hope of getting more custom. But the Church was of course where literacy flourished; hence the compilation of herbals and medical texts in monasteries. Practices that had been followed since the days of ancient Greece, such as picking herbs at a special time with chants and libations, were simply Christianized. The Pagan chants were replaced by the Lord's Prayer, the Creed or some other prayer.

Although the Church absorbed the main aspects of Anglo-Saxon magic, the Christian belief in a single, omnipotent God had an unfortunate effect on the teeming world of Pagan supernatural beings. All of them, from gods to dwarves, were

reclassified as devils. Thus any dealings with them were blasphemous, and even such innocent pastimes as casting lots fell under suspicion.

> *If anyone practices the lots which are reckoned disrespectful to the Saints, or indeed any kind of lots, or lots are cast under some evil influence, or if anyone makes divination, let them do penance for three years, one on bread and water.*

The Church frowned even more deeply upon magical efforts to control others, such as we have seen with love spells: "If anyone is a wizard, that is seeks to control someone's mind through the invoking of demons, let him do penance for five years, one on bread and water."

Such punishments seem lenient compared with the later death penalty for Satanic witchcraft; even the clergy – who appear to have been as culpable as anyone else – might lose their livelihood but escaped with their lives:

> *Those that consult divinations and use them in the Pagan manner, or that permit people of that kind into their houses to seek some knowledge of the evil art, or for the sake of averting some omen, they, if clergy, shall be expelled [from the Church]…*

To illustrate the rich confusion between Pagan magic and that of the Church, let us imagine for a moment the figure of St. Eanswythe, the daughter of King Eadbald. We recall that Eadbald returned to his Pagan beliefs before being persuaded back to Christianity; this was a period of considerable fluidity of belief. Eanswythe was a girl of determined character who when only 16 founded probably the first convent in England, at

Folkestone, in about 630 CE. Her legend records that she miraculously led a stream of water uphill to the convent for ease of access, and successfully ordered the birds not to eat the crops her nuns had sown. Such wonder stories would probably have first been circulated amongst local people before Church officials heard them and eventually declared them miracles. Eanswythe died, probably of the plague, around 650 CE.

We can picture the saint wearing an early type of nun's habit. From the belt hang a small crystal globe and a spoon with holes, along with keys and other useful items. She may wear a necklace of beads from which amulets hang. She is literate, able to read the Bible, prayers and divine services. The convent library may also possess herbals and medical manuscripts describing healing charms. Since the convent grows as much of its own food as possible, the kitchen garden will contain all the necessary herbs for healing, including the Nine Sacred Herbs. There will be hens to provide eggs for cooking and for binding herbal poultices and lotions. As a woman of the spirit and of authority, with access to her own church and all its blessings, Eanswythe will be the first person local people turn to for healing and blessing rituals, prophecies and divination.

We can imagine Eanswythe performing healing rituals, applying herbal remedies and invoking the Pagan gods along with the protection of Christ. She blesses the turfs that farmers bring her for the Land Ceremonies Charm. She performs exorcisms on those possessed by bad spirits. She and her nuns make herbal amulets on request. She will invoke divine protection upon those who are setting out on journeys, and help women with matters concerning conception and birth. She works healing magic over farm animals and chants to prevent bees from swarming.

This pioneering saint was also almost certainly a wise-woman working in the long-established Pagan tradition, because that was how she could best serve her people, and that is how they would have seen her. We know that pilgrimages to Eanswythe's relics were still popular during the mediaeval period, which suggests that in death, she continued to perform healing miracles for those who asked her.

With St. Eanswythe we have entered the world of Christianized Europe, slow and patchy though the conversion process was; Lithuania finally abandoned Paganism (officially) only in 1387.

Mediaeval Magic

As we move into the mediaeval period, we find that the growing power of Christianity caused a change in the way communities were arranged. Local churches were built, around which villages clustered. This marks the birth of what we think of as the traditional, typical English village. The ecclesiastical authority of the Church was matched by the manor house, which provided a focus of secular power. The comparative grandeur of church and manor house buildings underlined the inequalities of such a society, in which the majority of people owed taxes, produce and labour to a privileged few while they themselves underwent frequent shortages. Such conditions gave rise to magical practices focused on easing tough living conditions, siphoning off power from the institutions that claimed it. The mediaeval village

A magician casts a night-time spell for a military client, while the ominous sight of a bat is seen overhead.

> The Church had unwittingly created a spiritial vacuum by condemning the multitude of Anglo-Saxon otherworldly beings as demons. Ordinary people were quick to fill this vacuum with the figures of Christ and miracle-working saints. The Church itself was seen as essentially magical. Even the clergy were perceived as working magic during the Mass...

was bursting at the seams with magic. Working men and women might perform cures on their own family and livestock with charms and herbs, turning to a wise-man or woman when the situation demanded specific skills. The manor might house a learned magician privately working complex ceremonial magic. And the priest would be on hand with a rich variety of magical items and practices. As we have already seen, the Church was viewed 'as a vast reservoir of magical power, capable of being deployed for a variety of secular purposes.'

The Magical Church

The Church had unwittingly created a spiritual vacuum by condemning the multitude of Anglo-Saxon otherworldly beings as demons. Ordinary people were quick to fill this vacuum with the figures of Christ and miracle-working saints. The Church itself was seen as essentially magical. Even the clergy were perceived as working magic during the Mass, when they changed wine and bread into the blood and flesh of Christ. Nor were the clergy averse, as we have seen, to participating in overtly magical rituals either in the hallowed space of a church or outside. While the Church may have rigidly insisted that miracles and magic were two entirely different things – the first worked by holy saints, the second by unhallowed powers – such hair-splitting is likely to have been lost on people who were already happy mingling the names of Pagan gods with snatches of Christian prayer in their charms.

Every physical aspect of the Church became imbued with magical beliefs. Soil from a graveyard was full of magical power; a church-door key could protect against a mad dog; silver coins from the collection could cure illness; and, should it be possible to obtain one, a monk's scapular (a protective robe) would protect against the plague.

The Church itself provided magical charms in the form of medals or pieces of paper inscribed with the sign of the cross or gospel verses. Rosaries could be blessed to protect against fire, storms, illness and bad spirits. The *agnus dei* was a popular amulet – a small slab of wax made from paschal candles, blessed by the Pope and stamped with the lamb and flag. It was said to defend the wearer against 'the assaults of the Devil…thunder, lightning, fire, drowning, death in child-bed and similar dangers'.

If no talisman was available, the mere recitation of certain prayers could also prove effective. One could charm birds and snakes by the repetition of the correct Biblical verses, or find out the date of one's own death by reciting certain prayers to St. Brigid for 15 days. Maleficent magic could be worked by reciting prayers backwards; the Lord's Prayer was considered particularly effective.

The action of fasting was also imbued with magical power. Noting the weekday on which the Annunciation fell and fasting on that day for a year held sudden death at bay. Conversely, fasting could be used with the magical intention of causing an enemy's death.

The practice of using the Bible and other holy scriptures for divination had begun in the early days of Christianity, replacing the texts of Homer and Virgil that the Greeks and Romans had used in Pagan times. Some people would listen out for the passage being read at the moment they entered a church in order to divine the outcome of a situation. Once printing had made the scriptures more widely available (during the late 15th century), a copy of the Bible would be opened at random and a finger placed upon the page; this was known as the *sortes Biblicae*. Touching a Bible to a child's head would send it to sleep, and reading passages to a woman in labour ensured a successful birth.

Other Pagan practices were Christianized too, such as using magical springs. The Church re-dedicated these to various saints so that they became holy wells, but for the people little had changed. They still decorated the wells with flowers and used the water for divination and magical healing. The Church appropriated the festivals of the ritual year, but these, too, kept their Pagan feel. Yule, the winter solstice, became Christmas, although the traditional Yule log was maintained. May Day or Beltane became the Feast of Sts. Philip and James; Midsummer Eve that of John the Baptist. Many rituals that were traditionally observed on the Pagan festivals simply continued, such as the Beltane fires, between which cattle were driven to be purified. Observing the round of the ritual year was thought to guarantee good fortune, as well as offering opportunities for enjoyable communal celebrations.

As for the sacraments of the Church, they were thought to be so powerful that they were viewed with something like awe. The Mass itself, as we have seen, was a profoundly magical ritual in which the chanting of incomprehensible Latin words had the power to alter the substance of material objects. Simply attending the Mass was said to ensure that the day would be lived out

✝ *A picture dated c.1869 shows a blind girl visiting a holy well in the hope of a cure.*

without danger of death or sudden blindness. The wafer of bread given to communicants had so many magical uses that merely swallowing it seemed almost a waste. The communicant who went home with it could, for instance, grind it up and scatter it over the garden to repel caterpillars. Sneaking the wafer out of church was easy, because the priest simply placed it in the communicant's hand. Not until 1549 did instructions in the Book of Common Prayer order that it should be put directly into the mouth in order to avoid magical use. The wafer could be used to cure blindness or fever, put out fires, heal sick livestock, make an effective love charm, and so on. Churches were forced to keep the Eucharist and holy oil locked up, as well as putting locked lids over fonts to prevent the theft of holy water (useful for repelling witches and devils).

The Church itself was more than willing to celebrate masses for all kinds of benefits – to enhance easy travel or birth, ensure good weather or avert epidemics. Some priests did not even balk at magical attempts to hasten a person's death by performing masses for the dead while they were still alive. The grim ritual appears to have been worked without candles; the altar cloth was replaced with "doleful clothing" and thorns used to decorate the cross.

It is hard to escape the conclusion that the Church had got itself into a difficult position. After all, the authority of Christ and the saints depended upon the spiritual miracles they worked, and that of the Church itself derived from the same source of power, which was indistinguishable from magic. In setting up the figure of the Devil as a threat to all Christian souls, the Church was forced to provide spiritual protection that effectively competed with the charms and remedies that were provided by wise-men and women.

Everyone knew that demons caused the thunderstorms that endangered the crops, but the Church could put them to flight by ringing the bells or by parading the Host around the village. Holy water could be administered to a cow suffering bewitchment, and Christ himself had performed a spectacular exorcism on a man tormented by demons, setting a precedent for his clergy.

Quite apart from the holy items and services that could be put to magical use were the objects supplied by the priesthood that did not originate with the Church. Such is the Harley Roll, a strip of parchment painted with a complex scheme of diagrams, prayers, invocations and benedictions laid out according to measurements relating to the instruments of Christ's passion. The whole roll is the same length as Christ's body was reputed to be. This extraordinary object, which dates from the 15th century, must have been custom made, although it cannot be related to any practice or worship sanctioned by the Church. Inscriptions upon it promise protection from a range of ills: insomnia, sudden death, attack or accident while travelling, thunder and lightning, enemies and evil spirits. A prayer to saints Julitta and Quirricus, who were mother and child, suggests that it could also be used as a birth girdle, to be wrapped around the body of a woman in labour. Any clergyman owning such an all-purpose item would be in constant demand.

Magical manuscripts made for specific purposes were also in circulation. One in particular, known as Abraham's Eye, had been in use for catching thieves since at least the 4th century, and was still popular in mediaeval times. The design centred on an eye within a circle, together with images of a key, hammer or knife and the names of various angels. The manuscript would be displayed in a public place where the thief was likely to be present; prayers were recited over it and then either a knife or a key used to pierce the eye. At that point the thief would be revealed by their cry of agony.

Similarly blurring the line between religion and magic was the concentration of practices designed to deal with the dangers faced both by, and from, the dead. Protection for a corpse could be provided by placing a pilgrim's token in the coffin as the soul set off on its final journey. Other items were sometimes slipped in, such as lead tablets engraved with scriptural verses or magical charms. Not all the dead slept easily, though, and revenants were feared.

The clergy themselves might endanger the living. William of Newburgh was a 12th-century Augustinian canon and historian; he recorded the tale of a priest who, bad in life, rose from his grave nightly until his colleagues attacked him with an axe. When they checked his grave later, the corpse was seen to have a fresh wound, still bleeding.

Ceremonial Magic

While the priests and wise-men and women plied their trades down in the village, in the manor house the lord of the manor might be attempting to contact angels in order to receive staggering amounts of knowledge unavailable by natural means. Considerable learning was required for this kind of magic and also the means to obtain the necessary manuscripts, such as the 11th-century Arabic compendium of magic and astrology, *Picatrix*. The 13th-century *Ars Notoria* offered methods for obtaining knowledge instantly and completely. Such desirable rewards were not easily won; the mage had to undergo lengthy purifications before facing spiritual beings that ranged from angels to demons. The latter posed both physical and spiritual dangers, so the mage had to be sure he was well protected. The Church of course frowned upon any deliberate contact with demonic forces, which had therefore to be pursued in secret. The outspoken 13th-century Italian mage and astrologer Cecco

Protection for a corpse could be provided by placing a pilgrim's token in the coffin as the soul set off on its final journey.

d'Ascoli paid with his life for describing rituals employing demons and for attempting to calculate Christ's horoscope, harmless though the latter endeavour might seem to us. He was burned at the stake in Florence in 1327, at the age of 70.

The world of magic had developed and changed since Anglo-Saxon times, as the Church claimed the authority to outlaw and condemn practices outside its own jurisdiction while simultaneously offering comparable remedies and methods of protection. In the British Isles and Europe, the rich mixture of magic drew upon many sources stretching back to the worlds of Greece and Rome, together with gods and beliefs spread by the Angles, Saxons and Vikings, Celtic beliefs and the occasional outcrop of learned magic deriving from Arabic sources. It would not be long before the broth came to the boil.

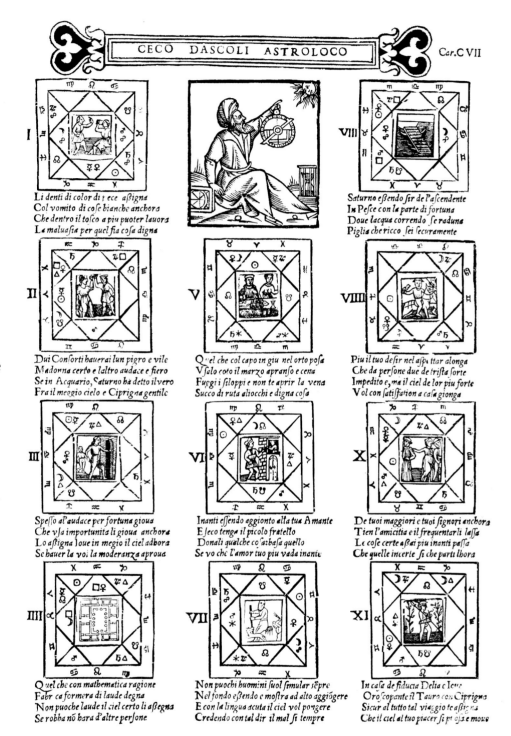

 Table with astrologer Cecco d'Ascoli, from Triumph of fortune, By Sigismondo Fanti Ferrarese, Venice, 1526, Italy.

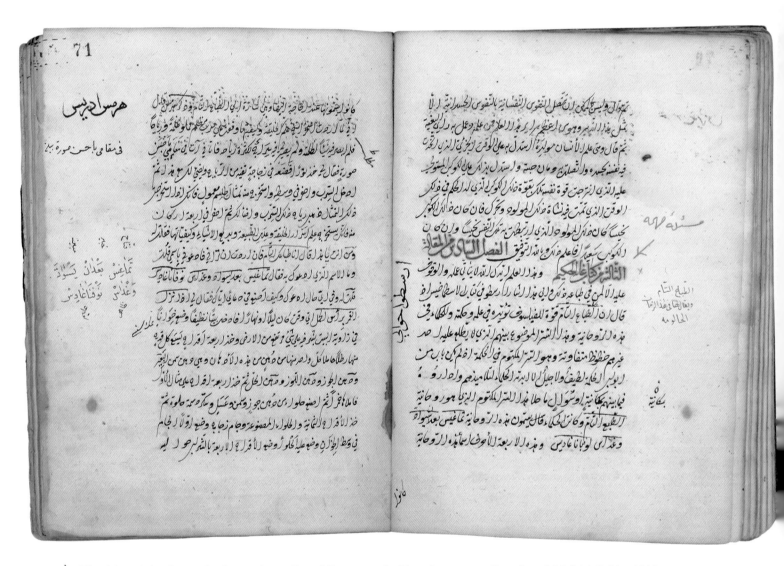

The Aim of the Sage, *also known in mediaeval Europe as the* Picatrix, *was attributed to al-Majriti, Jedda, 1566.*

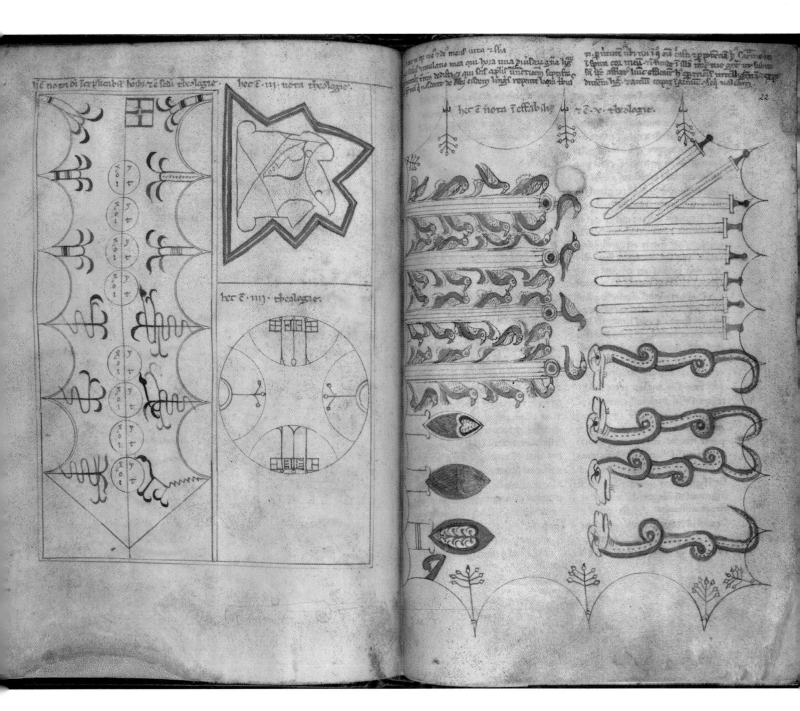

Sloane manuscript of Ars notoria Salomonis, Machinei et Euclidis *from* Membranaceus.

Chapter Three

Glamorous Witches and Hungry Women

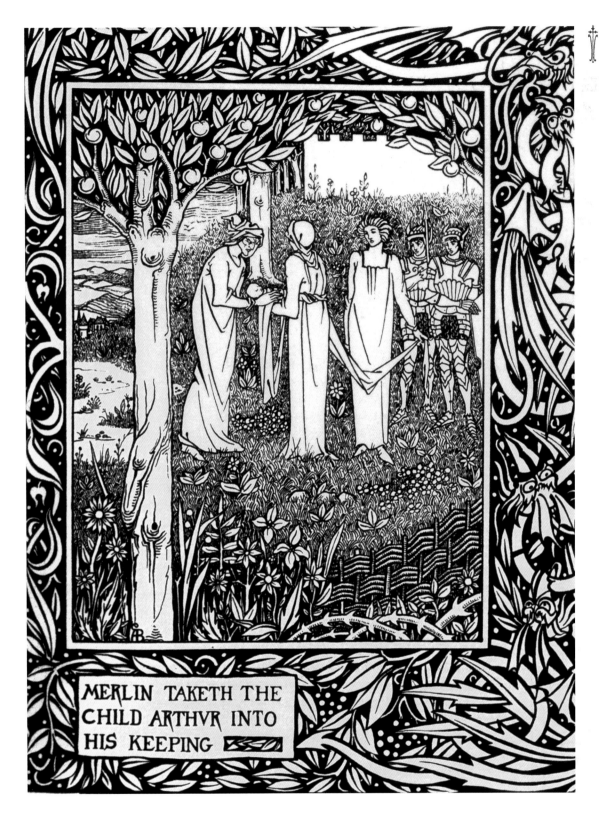

MERLIN TAKETH THE CHILD ARTHVR INTO HIS KEEPING

Illustration by Aubrey Beardsley for Malory's Le Morte D'Arthur, *showing Merlin taking charge of baby Arthur.*

Arthurian Magic

EUROPE AND GREAT BRITAIN in mediaeval times were thoroughly Christian, with the Catholic Church dominating life in both town and country. However, a strong undercurrent of older beliefs and practices continued to flow through life, remnants of which can be experienced even in the present day. You already know that in attempting to expunge Pagan magical practices, the Church itself became viewed as powerfully magical. Since magic was so thoroughly woven into ordinary life, it is hardly surprising that the mythology of Great Britain is deeply involved with it.

The Matter of Britain is one of three great mediaeval legendary cycles, the others being the Matter of France and the Matter of Rome. The British cycle consists of literature that sets out and elaborates on the history of the mythical King Arthur and other, less memorable, kings. It also covers tales of Brittany, which Anglo-Saxons had colonized during the fifth and sixth centuries and which was known as Lesser Britain.

Although the Arthurian tales are imbued with Christianity, as evidenced by the story of the Grail, magic is never seen as being inspired by the Devil. That outlook would come later, and we shall see how it developed during the course of this chapter. Rather, Arthurian magic is a literary device that spices up the tales of chivalry with wonder and danger. When Arthur sat down to feast on great occasions, such as Christmas, he was in the habit of refusing to eat until he had seen some wonder or other; thus the virtuous observations of the Christian festivals and the acknowledgement of the world of magic sat comfortably side by side.

> …a strong undercurrent of older beliefs and practices continued to flow through life, remnants of which can be experienced even today.

Merlin the Magician

In a sense, the whole Arthurian cycle is set in motion by one figure: Merlin the magician. By the time Sir Thomas Malory came to write his version of the legend, *Le Morte d'Arthur* (published in 1485), he was confident enough that readers would know who Merlin was to introduce him in the first chapter without any explanation or description. It is Merlin who engineers Arthur's birth and parentage, disguising the lovelorn Uther Pendragon as the husband of the virtuous Igraine so that she accepts him as her lover. Merlin's price for this service is to be given the child born of the union, so Arthur is brought up under magical

The Battle of the red and white dragons, with the red representing Britons and the white the Saxons. King Vortigern and Merlin look on.

tutelage. Arthur wins the throne of Britain by a feat so famous we tend to forget it is magical: he pulls from a stone a sword that no other contestant can budge. Merlin then acts as his advisor for a while, until he vanishes from the scene.

Merlin's biographer – for such we may call him – was the 12th-century cleric and historian Geoffrey of Monmouth. Geoffrey wrote a history of the kings of Britain, as well as a life of Merlin and a book of his prophecies. However, his idea of history was a good deal more fantastical than the sober reporting of facts that we consider history to be.

According to Geoffrey, a minor British king, Vortigern, was attempting to build a fort he could defend against the Saxons, but every night the building work would be torn down. Vortigern's Druid advisors tell him that he must sacrifice a fatherless child in the foundations, and his soldiers discover young Merlin, fathered on a Welsh princess by a supernatural being. Merlin avoids an untimely death by explaining to Vortigern that a red and a white dragon fighting amongst the foundations are destroying his building work. Vortigern investigates and when the dragons have been found and immobilized, Merlin bursts forth into prophecy, promising that 'the boar of Cornwall' will put the Saxons to flight. The boar is, of course, King Arthur.

Merlin then goes off to move a circle of gigantic stones from Ireland to Salisbury Plain to serve as a royal mausoleum, thus creating Stonehenge. Many other legends gather around Merlin, including his fatal infatuation with the glamorous but heartless Nimue, one of the Ladies of the Lake. She sweet-talks him into teaching her all his magical secrets, only to imprison him forever under a huge stone – a neat reversal of King Arthur's freeing of the

sword. However, other versions of Merlin's story describe a happier fate, with Merlin choosing to withdraw from the world into a high tower together with his learned sister Ganeida, there to study the stars and discuss philosophy.

The Sword from the Lake

The linking of Merlin with Stonehenge suggests that these stories belong in an unimaginably distant past, and in fact there are other archaic traces in the Arthurian cycle that give hints of the antiquity of the legends. Take for example Arthur's sword, Excalibur.

Swords had been given names at least since Anglo-Saxon times, indicating that they were in some sense thought to be alive. But the origins of Excalibur could be a great deal older than that. The Arthurian myth tells that, as he lies dying after his final battle, Arthur instructs his attendant Sir Bedivere to throw the sword into the nearby lake. Sir Bedivere, reluctant to waste such a valuable weapon, disobeys him twice, hiding the sword instead of acting as instructed. But Arthur realizes what he has done and reprimands him, so that on the magical third time Bedivere finally flings Excalibur far out into the lake. A hand rises above the water, seizes the sword, and waves it three times. Thus Excalibur returns to the Lady of the Lake, from whom (in some versions of the legend) Arthur had originally received it.

You have already learned that the practice of casting weapons into streams or lakes had been followed since before metals were discovered, and the practice continued into the Bronze and Iron Ages. Swords would be disabled or perhaps symbolically killed by bending or breaking before being "drowned." An ancient magical practice has become one of the most memorable images of the legend of the greatest (mythical) king of Britain.

The Once and Future King

The death of Arthur as recounted by Malory is an ambiguous confusion of frankly magical Pagan elements glossed over with a little Christian imagery. After Sir Bedivere has disposed of Excalibur, he carries Arthur to the water's edge, where a barge full of noble ladies awaits him. There are three queens amongst the ladies, including Arthur's half-sister, Morgan le Fay, who, like Nimue (who is also on the barge), learned sorcery from Merlin. Despite both Morgan and Nimue appearing earlier in the epic as enemies to Arthur and Merlin, at this supreme point in the tale they are healers who take the king to the Vale of Avalon, where they can restore him to health.

However, Arthur's fate is uncertain. The next day, Bedivere comes across a chapel in a clearing near Glastonbury where a hermit is praying by a newly carved tomb that he explains holds the body of a man brought in at midnight by a group of women. Bedivere realizes that this is Arthur's

After Sir Bedivere has disposed of Excalibur, he carries Arthur to the water's edge, where a barge full of noble ladies awaits him. There are three queens amongst the ladies, including Arthur's half-sister, Morgan le Fay, who, like Nimue, learned sorcery from Merlin. At this supreme point in the tale, they are healers who take the king to the Vale of Avalon....

Excalibur given to King Arthur by the Lady of the Lake.

A painting by Frank William Warwick Topham (1838-1924) depicts the voyage of King Arthur and Morgan le Fay to the Isle of Avalon.

tomb, and resolves to stay there always to pray for his king's soul.

The anonymity of the buried man allows Malory to throw doubt on the story after telling it, and to suggest that Arthur might after all have been healed in Avalon. But then he becomes cautious, attributing the idea of Avalon to hearsay. He takes care to introduce Christian elements that sit uneasily with the idea of a man being preserved from death in order to serve his country again.

> *Yet some men say in many parts of England that King Arthur is not dead, but had by the will of our Lord Jesu into another place; and men say that he shall come again, and he shall win the holy cross. I will not say it shall be so, but rather I will say, here in this world he changed his life. But many men say that there is written upon his tomb this verse: Hic jacet Arthurus Rex, quondam Rex que futurus.*

The inscription states, 'Here lies King Arthur, the once and future king'. The implication is that Arthur will return to lead his nation in a time of great need; in other words, he is no longer a man but a supernatural being who waits to live out his fate rather than dying and going to the Christian heaven. This idea is so profoundly embedded in the British mind that it still tends to be evoked at times of crisis. Christ may save individual souls, but it takes a magical king to save the country.

A Game of Beheading

A thread of ambiguity runs throughout the Matter of Britain. Are Morgan le Fay and Nimue healers or evil sorceresses? Is the culture of Camelot Christian or Pagan? Both these questions occur during one of the most famous stories of the Knights of the Round Table, that of Sir Gawain and the Green Knight. Although the story does not appear in Malory, a narrative poem was written about it in the late 14th century.

The tale is of a magical challenge. About to feast at New Year, Arthur (as is his habit) wishes to see or hear some marvel before he will start eating. Right on cue, a gigantic man rides into the hall, green all over – even down to his horse. He asks for a volunteer to strike him a single blow with his axe, on the understanding that he will return the blow a year later. Sir Gawain accepts the challenge and strikes off the giant's head. However, the green knight simply picks up his head, reminds Gawain of the terms of the game, and rides off.

As New Year draws near once again, Gawain prepares to meet the giant at the Green Chapel. He is fitted out with armour, including a shield bearing a pentangle in gold. This is the first appearance of the word "pentangle" in English. This five-pointed "endless knot" was reputed to have been engraved on a magical ring with which King Solomon controlled demons; it thus passed into ritual magic as a powerful device, and its appearance on a Christian knight's shield is unexpected. The anonymous poet clearly realizes this, for he expends a lot of lines and effort in

The Green Knight, on his green horse, surprises Arthur and Guinevere at a feast. He later challenges the knights to a fight and Gawain, who volunteered, was victorious.

coming up with various rather unconvincing interpretations, such as that Gawain possessed five virtues, Christ had five wounds, and so on. But the pentangle is, first and foremost, a magical symbol.

When Gawain arrives at the Green Chapel, the Green Knight, along with his beautiful wife and an old woman, welcomes him. They overwhelm him with hospitality, which, to Gawain's alarm, includes the lady attempting to seduce him. Twice he accepts no more than a kiss from her, but the third time she offers him a protective girdle, and he cannot resist taking it to wear when he suffers his blow from the Knight.

The magical girdle is an image that can be traced back as far as ancient Greece. Aphrodite had a girdle that inspired love, and the sea nymph Leucothea gave Odysseus her veil to wrap around his waist; he could not drown or be injured while wearing it. As described in the previous chapter, in everyday life girdles inscribed with prayers and magical symbols were used for healing illness and easing childbirth.

The tale ends with Gawain's escape from certain death, but there is one final surprise: the whole situation has been engineered by Morgan le Fay to test one of Arthur's knights and to frighten Guinevere to death at the New Year feast. This tale, with its folk motif of magical challenges, symbols from myth and magic, and the ambiguous presence of a sorceress who has both noble and evil motivations, typifies the otherworldly atmosphere of the Matter of Britain.

The Cunning Folk

While ancient magical practices were being preserved in the world of literature, quite different strands of activity were developing among ordinary people. By the 13th century, those semi-professional sorcerers who worked in their local communities had become known as cunning folk. They used both folk magic and herb lore together with local knowledge and a good dash of psychological insight. Those who knew only a single spell were known as charmers. Usually the charmers' knowledge was passed down a family, sometimes being revealed on a deathbed. Charmers were not allowed to charge for their services, although they might accept payment indirectly, in kind; cunning folk expected payment for their services.

Simple charming of skin ailments such as warts has been proved to work, since the central nervous system and immune system often respond to powerful suggestions of healing. Charming was often done with an amulet, hundreds of which survive. The spells upon them are full of the names of saints, drafted in to perform traditional, pre-Christian cures.

Apart from healing, the cunning folk boasted a comprehensive body of magical techniques, offering a range of services from removing curses to finding stolen goods. Some cunning folk specialized in a certain area, such as love magic. They charged for their services according to the complexity of each job, but cunning was only ever a sideline, being an uncertain source of income. Cunning folk could come from the lower end of the social scale but also appeared on the level of tradespeople and the like; they were to be found in villages but also thrived in towns, where they could be certain of finding many clients. Some became so well known for their skill that people would travel long distances to visit them.

Cunning depended on abilities to innovate according to need, use the imagination, and also have some basic grasp of how human nature works. For example, someone who was suffering a run of bad luck might decide an enemy had cursed them, and go to a cunning person to have the curse removed. The remedy might include a counter-curse to harm or bind the aggressor, worked by making an image of the person and piercing it with pins. The more dramatic the

Cunning depended on abilities to innvoate according to need, use the imagination, and also have some basic grasp of how human nature works.

performance, the more confident the victim would feel that it would work. We should remember that there were few other sources of help to which people could turn. Medical doctors were expensive and their treatments often ineffective, and there was no police force to find and catch thieves or locate stolen goods.

Witch Marks, Bottles, Cats and Middens

We have already looked at some of the ways in which the magical power of the Church was used for protection and healing. But that is not all; from the 11th century onwards, a new form of protection began to appear in churches right across Europe. People marked the structure of the building itself with magical symbols, now known as witch marks, although the term is misleading. These marks are scratched into the plaster on the inner walls of the church, or in stonework around doors and windows, and even on metal locks. The simplest may have been created with a pair of shears, a common household item.

A wide variety of patterns has so far come to light, and they vary surprisingly little across the huge distances between Britain and Eastern Europe. One of the most common is known as the daisy wheel, which is formed of six petals inside a circle. Others include two interlinked V's, overlapping circles, and squares with lines running from corner to corner. There are simple straight lines that could easily be scratched, as well as complex maze patterns that would have required considerable time and skill to make.

These enigmatic marks have only recently come to the attention of archaeologists, and since there is no written explanation of them, their meaning is obscure. However, it has been conjectured that they are intended to protect the church from evil forces. Patterns tend to cluster around points of entry such as doors and windows, or places of concentrated spiritual power such as the font. The daisy-wheel pattern had been in use since Roman times, but in contrast it is thought that the double

V refers to Christ's mother as *virgin virginorum* – virgin of virgins. If this is so, then no distinction is made between pre-Christian and Christian magical efficacy. What's more, these marks would originally have been highly visible since they were scratched through what was once brightly coloured plaster, right down to the stone. No record survives of any objections from the clergy, who must have accepted their congregation's right to participate in worship in this unusual way. Since services were conducted in Latin, perhaps people felt that the only way they could take an

Ancient witch marks carved into stone on an English medieval door frame, from the 15th century, to keep witches out.

A daisy wheel witch mark in a 16th century Herefordshire house. This protective sign has been carved into a wooden beam and rubbed with white lime to make it more visible.

active part in the working of magic in the church was by non-verbal means.

Why were churches singled out as needing particular protection? There are two possible answers. The first is that the forces of evil would naturally concentrate their malevolence on places of great spiritual power. The second is that it's very possible that houses were marked in the same way; we cannot tell this because hardly any domestic buildings survive from before the 16th century, being mostly made of fragile wattle and daub.

During the 16th and 17th centuries, a process known as "The Great Rebuild" changed the nature of domestic housing. Stone chimneys were inserted and rooms 'ceiled' to create an upper floor; the inner space was divided into more rooms, and voids were created alongside the chimney or around the joists.

The more durable materials used – stone, wood and brick – have of course lasted much longer than wattle and daub. Where such houses have survived, they, like churches, have witch marks etched into the fabric. As in the churches, patterns gather around doors and windows, but also in other vulnerable areas. Fireplaces receive attention, as do dark areas and also some pieces of furniture. Witch marks map out what individuals or families considered most in need of protection. It's logical to suppose that people, too, carried protective devices, probably in the form of amulets.

Witch marks were not the only kind of magic being worked in the home. Along with people and furniture, houses held secret deposits of various kinds of items. Renovation works on old buildings often reveal objects buried under thresholds, alongside windows, beneath the hearth and floors,

in chimneys, in cavities of ceiling, wall or attic, and in thatch. It seems that any area of entry or exit and also unused voids were feared as spaces where unwanted forces might find their way into the house or perhaps settle down and stay.

An ancient protective practice involved the inclusion of animal remains in the structure of the house. The most popular choice was a dried cat; by 2004, about 100 had been discovered in British houses. Sometimes the cat's legs were bound, while others were posed as if chasing or attacking; a few were even accompanied by a dried rat. Perhaps a mummified cat protected the house against vermin, or perhaps its nocturnal habits suggested that it could seek out and repel malevolent spirits. Cats are also small enough to be easily concealed.

Mummified cats may be disturbing to the modern eye, but these houses were also bursting with hidden inanimate objects. Commonly found are witch bottles; rather than belonging to witches they were intended to ward off malevolent magic. Usually they are found buried beneath the hearth or threshold, but sometimes beneath floorboards or in walls. Over 200 have been found in England. Most of these are of a type known as Bellamine, a narrow-necked, bulbous bottle decorated with a bearded face. When opened, such bottles reveal intimate objects such as hair and nail clippings and traces of urine, together with thorns, pins or nails. Thus equipped and buried in house or garden, they protected the individual involved against malevolent magic; the sharp objects would pierce and injure anyone aiming ill will at the owner of the clippings and urine.

Witch bottles could also be used actively against witches, if an item in the Pitt Rivers Museum in Oxford is trustworthy. This is a small

✝ *Concealed shoes found in East Anglia that are thought to have been 'spiritual midden'.*

glass bottle, stoppered, and allegedly containing a witch. Presumably the dangerous work of trapping a witch would have been carried out by a professional cunning person.

Other bottles may contain love spells, since fabric hearts have also been found in some of them. Such a bottle might act to catch and hold a lover's attention for as long as it remained safely concealed. Perhaps if the lover was no longer

wanted, the bottle would be smashed and the contents burned.

Rather more mysterious than the witch bottle is the cache of old clothes and shoes dubbed "spiritual midden." Like witch marks, these deposits have received scholarly attention only recently. The practice of hiding such personal items goes back at least to the 16th century and may be older. Caches are found in voids around chimneys or in walls created by lathe-and-plaster work, and some of them are quite large. Like witch marks, they have been found wherever Europeans settled, from North America to Tasmania. Most middens are made up of personal items such as worn-out clothes and shoes. However, others contain seemingly random objects: animal bones, notched sticks, almanacs. Others contain only well-worn shoes, usually odd ones. For some reason, shoe middens are always found near a hearth, though by the 19th century they also appear under floorboards and in ceilings.

Such middens built up over many years, with items apparently being added by each generation.

What might be the function of such caches? Each object included must have had some significance, which is easy to see in the case of clothing and shoes but less so with the other items. Does a pig's trotter merit inclusion because something important happened at one particular pig-sticking or pork dinner? Sadly, no historical person appears to have kept a diary or written a letter saying, "Today I dumped my old woollen skirt and some chicken bones in the chimney. Now I feel properly protected against malevolent spells against myself or my poultry." Archaeologists can only speculate that such middens were thought to have the power of averting evil influences, like the witch marks and bottles.

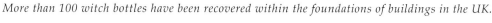 *More than 100 witch bottles have been recovered within the foundations of buildings in the UK.*

The custom endured for so long that it is quite possible that eventually nobody remembered why they were disposing of various pieces of rubbish in such a handy way. Right up until the mid-20th century, some builders in local companies would still include a ritual item in a newly built house, "for luck."

How the Witch Came to Be

The question that arises from all this apotropaic activity is: what frightened people so much? The answer is, of course, the witch. As already noted, ever since ancient times there had been a tendency to blame misfortunes such as illness, accidents and crop failure on supernatural causes. Large-scale catastrophes such as epidemics could be seen as punishments from the gods, requiring propitiation by ritual and sacrifice. Individual runs of bad luck were more likely to be put down to an enemy's curses. Thus, by the early mediaeval period, the witch began to take her place alongside the village cunning person. In theory, people would go to the cunning person for help and healing, and to the witch for vengeful curses. But did the witch really exist?

As you have learned, belief in witchcraft goes back to the ancient world and possibly beyond, into prehistory. On the other hand, the actual existence of malevolent witches seems to be confined to the pages of literature. Magic was woven into the fabric of life as a means of dealing with illness and daily problems, and such benevolent charms can be read in the likes of *Bald's Leechbook*. However, the only written evidence of curses that survives comes from the lead curse tablets produced during the Roman occupation, which were made by ordinary people. By mediaeval times, if anyone wished to blight crops or cause neighbours or their livestock to sicken or die, they would turn to a cunning person.

Several factors come together to create the image of the embittered, evil-doing witch. The first is Christianity. As described in Chapter Two, the Church's relationship with magic was ambivalent; in theory, it condemned all magical practices while blandly offering many of its own magical protective and healing techniques. But at a certain point in time and place, that attitude hardened so that all and any magic worked without the approval of the Church was branded as inspired by demons – that is, satanic. Perhaps surprisingly, this time and place has been pinpointed: the early 15th century, in the mountains of the Alps and the Pyrenees. Here was sounded the first tremor of alarm leading to the insanity of the witch trials that gripped Europe and Britain for three long, cruel centuries, eventually affecting America as well.

The Church at this time was increasingly concerned with the problem posed by heretical sects such as the Cathars and Waldensians. Such sects sought a return to a life of purity, and implicitly rejected the Church's authority in favour of their own inspired leaders. The Church could not tolerate such a challenge, and official persecution drove many heretical groups into the Pyrenees and Alps. Leading lights of the two great preaching orders of monks, the Dominicans and

A depiction from the 15th century shows a witch, accompanied by a beggar and a fool, cursing two sergeants-at-arms who slink away terrified.

the Franciscans, fulminated against both heresy and magic as being inspired by the Devil, so it is hardly surprising that the two became confused in people's minds. In 1424, in the Abreu Valley of the Pyrenees, local people were accused of going out by night to worship the Devil in the company of *bruxas* – nocturnal child-killing demons feared since Roman times. Eventually the term came to mean *witches*. Thus the basic elements of the Devil-worshipping, night-travelling group of witches were established. However, the charge was not witchcraft but heresy, and this continued to be the case on the Continent throughout the course of the witch-trial craze.

The heretical sects were also believed to gather in groups to worship the Devil. They were accused of murdering and eating children, and of indulging in nocturnal orgies. Such charges were positively clichéd, having been hurled since ancient times against Jews, Christians, Gnostics and any other set of believers whose existence appeared to threaten those in authority. Naturally enough, the same things were believed of witches. Both heretical sects and witches were feared because the Church's viewpoint echoed folkloric fears of wicked beings, producing a terrifying image of organized groups of satanic evildoers endowed with supernatural powers. Witches could take the form of wolves to attack sheep or become invisible; they murdered children and ate the corpses, blighted crops, stole milk from cows, paralyzed or blinded the able-bodied, and caused illness and miscarriages. They worshiped the Devil, who, appearing as an animal, gave them all the above powers. Worst of all – and this was a new charge – was that they entered into a pact with the Devil, usually signed in blood. The ascetic heretic, the helpful cunning person, the

> Both heretical sects and witches were feared because the Church's viewpoint echoed folkloric fears of wicked beings, producing a terrifying image of organized groups of satanic evildoers...

midwife, or anyone seen performing a simple magical act – all these innocent people were viewed through a new lens that changed them into satanic witches.

Key to this image is the idea of conspiracy, the third factor in the creation of the witch-trial craze. Today we are familiar with conspiracy theories, and may think they're a modern phenomenon, but they were in full bloom during the mediaeval period. Various minority groups – Jews, Muslims,

The notorious German witch-finder, Konrad von Marburg, sends another victim to the torture-chamber and the stake.

lepers, beggars – at one time or another all came under suspicion of plotting to kill innocent Christians, usually by poisoning wells. Some who were accused confessed under torture, once they had learned what they were expected to say. The persecution of witches is another strand of this mass paranoia that spread across Western Europe to the destruction of not only thousands of individual lives but also whole communities.

Night Flyers and Virtuous Werewolves

Other groups of people who held somewhat unorthodox beliefs were targeted and forced into the mould of the imaginary evildoing witch. Perhaps the best known is that of the *benandanti*, the trial records of whom were uncovered during the 1960s by historian Carlo Ginzburg. The *benandanti* (the 'Good Walkers') appear to have been known only in Friuli, in the northeastern corner of Italy. What distinguished these people was that each had been born with a caul. It was believed that this gave them the power to leave their bodies by night and fly in spirit to do battle with witches (the *malandanti*) and evil spirits that constantly threatened to harm the crops. Such trance flights took place on Thursday nights during the Ember Days – days set aside for prayer and fasting four times a year during the Church calendar.

Both men and women could become *benandanti*. Together they took on the vital business of fighting witches, often flying to the battles in the shape of

animals such as cats, mice or rabbits. After such battles, they reported drinking wine in the houses of the rich. Bad witches did the same thing, but would urinate in the casks after drinking their fill. All these people were involved in agriculture; their lives depended on their crops and livestock, and during periods of hardship they went hungry. Their trance flights clearly reflect the urgency of their needs, how close they lived to starvation. *Benandanti* were also believed to have healing powers, so all in all they were valuable members of their communities.

Unfortunately this amiable group of people came to the attention of the Inquisition at Rome. Alerted by the local priest, the first inquisitorial investigation in 1575 appears to have concluded that the *benandanti* were merely imagining their night flights and fights with witches. However, five years later another inquisitor decided to reopen investigations. This time the original informant, Paolo Gasparotto, panicked and denied he'd ever been a *benandanti*, but another man stepped forward and described the night flights and battles. Gasparotto then admitted that he'd been afraid that if he confessed the truth, the witches would beat him up. Neither of the men feared the Inquisition at this point, as they were firm in their conviction that they were going about Christ's business, defending the innocent against evil forces.

Such a mixture of folkloric practice and Christian belief was difficult for inquisitors to understand, since in the eyes of the Church any magic not given official sanction was the work of the Devil. Repeated interrogations ensued, and more people were drawn into the case; women who saw the dead and carried messages from them to the living, or who knew a few healing

Not all werewolves were evil; some fought witches by night in order to secure a good harvest and protect communities from harm.

The Sabbat of the Witches, *painted by Hans Baldung Grien, circa 1508–10.*

charms and used them locally. All fell under suspicion of Devil worship, no matter how firmly they denied it.

A document of canon law, the *Canon Episcopi,* had in the 10th century laid down that night rides were an illusion caused by the Devil; however, here were people who were convinced they flew by night, regularly, and for virtuous reasons. Therefore, the inquisitors felt sure that the *benandanti* and the healers were enslaved by the Devil's power. Under relentless questioning, some of the accused changed their stories until they finally realized what was required of them: to confess that they were witches.

The *benandanti* were not the only group living a secret and exciting life by night; others were

Theiss told his judges that he was a werewolf but he fought the witches on certain nights of the year to protect the crops.

engaged in the fight against evil forces that threatened the food supply. In eastern Europe, an area bordering the Baltic Sea known as Livonia was home to night-roaming werewolves. But these were not the evil creatures of legend. In 1692 a man in his eighties, Thiess, was tried for heresy. Thiess told his judges that he was a werewolf but (like the *benandanti*) he fought witches on certain nights of the year to protect the crops. His story was that he and other werewolves ventured down into hell on St. Lucy's Night, Pentecost and St. John's. There they fought the Devil and witches with iron rods. The fighting was fierce; Thiess attributed his broken nose to a witch called Skeistan, a fellow peasant who had died some time ago but whose strength was clearly unimpaired by that trifling fact.

Thiess was convinced that his company of wolves performed a crucial task; they assured the year's supply of food by bringing back grain and buds from hell. If they delayed their raid, they might find hell's gates barred, in which case the harvest would be poor. He described the werewolves more than once as the hounds of God. Other werewolves performed the same service in both Germany and Russia. As with the *benandanti*, such an idea flew in the face of all that the good Christian judges believed, and they tried hard to force Thiess to confess that he served the Devil. Thiess stuck to his guns, even boasting that what he achieved was more useful than anything his local priest might do – a valid point, since he ensured his community did not starve. He was sentenced to ten lashes of the whip.

The werewolves padded down to hell along the ground, but the *benandanti* were not the only groups of people taking to the night skies for tranced flights. It is not possible to say how old the practice was. The Synod of Ancyra, held in 314, decreed against women who flew on animals through the night sky in Diana's retinue. That doesn't seem to have stopped them, though, as in the 10th century an Italian abbot, Regino of Prüm, fulminated against women who believed that they joined the entourage of the Roman goddess Diana in night flights. Diana, a virgin goddess, shunned the company of men, so these flights were strictly female-only gatherings. In the aforementioned *Canon Episcopi* Regino condemned these events as illusions created by the Devil.

Four centuries later, the theologian William of Auvergne gave his learned opinion about a belief of the common people that a divine being called Abundia or Satia would lead her followers through various rich houses and their cellars. If offerings of food and drink had been left out, she would bless the house with prosperity; if not, she withdrew her protection. In either case, she and her retinue would feast upon whatever food and wine they could find. The authors of the 13th-century poem *Le Roman de la Rose* also alluded to dame Abonde. Her followers consisted of the third child in every family, who was qualified to follow the lady three times a week to enjoy the nocturnal hospitality of neighbouring houses. Like the *benandanti* and Diana's retinue, they travelled in spirit, leaving their bodies asleep in their beds. The belief was commonly held that the soul would be unable to return to its body should anyone turn over the latter. The ecstatic night flight was not without its perils, and other dangers were soon to appear.

These delightful night flights were still occurring in Italy in the 14th century, when two Milanese women were accused of attending supernatural meetings of the Society of Signora Oriente. Sibilla Zanni and Pierina de' Bugatis confessed to going out every Thursday with the society, paying homage to Diana and feasting on every kind of animal except the ass, which was sacred to Christ. Sibilla had attended such meetings since childhood, and both of them refused to believe they were behaving in any way contrary to the Church's teachings. They were, however, forced to promise that they would mend their ways.

Six years later, someone reported them as having relapsed, and this time the case was

Women join the retinue of the goddess Diana and fly through the night sky.

During the Inquisition, Carlos II, ruler of Spain, at age 19, watches the burning of heretics at Madrid.

referred to the Inquisition. Thus their testimony was guided and warped until it fell into a familiar pattern; they had signed a pact with the Devil in their own blood and called upon demons to fly them to the diabolical meetings. Both were found guilty and both of the women – who had innocently inherited an ancient dream of freedom and plenty – were executed.

It is probable that the name of Diana, as perhaps also Abundia, was bestowed by the educated men who wrote about this phenomenon. Other names for the night-flying goddess are

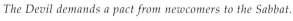 *The Devil demands a pact from newcomers to the Sabbat.*

Pre-Christian goddesses such as Frau Perchta also led ecstatic nighttime rides through the sky.

known; in Germany the common people knew her as Frau Perchta or Frau Holle. Classicizing the name was one way that learned men such as judges sought to grapple with a practice that was utterly strange to them and needed to be brought within the Christian worldview. All Pagan doings were, by definition, demonically inspired. Such an outlook stood in opposition to the understanding of those actually involved in nocturnal spirit journeys, as we have seen with Thiess. They were firm in their conviction that they were doing good, protecting the food supply and rewarding those who kept their houses in good order and who correctly left offerings for friendly spirits.

The focus on food in all these nocturnal ramblings speaks volumes. Those who left their human bodies behind to fly or trot through the night were hungry. They were fixated on making sure that they, and their communities, would have enough to eat and drink in the future. They were performing practical acts on behalf of those with whom they lived and worked. And, in the case of Diana's women, they were enjoying a freedom impossible in their daily lives. But neither secular judges nor those of the Inquisition saw it that way.

What Caused the Witch-Trial Craze?

It has been said that the history of witchcraft in Europe is that of a concept that bore very little resemblance to reality. So powerful a grip on the public imagination had that concept that the craze lasted for over three centuries, with the first known trials taking place in 1424 and the last in Switzerland in 1782. Historian Ronald Hutton has estimated that during those three centuries, between 40,000 and 60,000 people were burned or hanged. Earlier estimates had set the upper figure at 100,000. According to Hutton, the worst period was between 1560 and 1640, when the Reformation was causing extreme religious tension to the point of war.

Several causes for this mass insanity have been proposed. The paranoid fear of conspiracy, projected upon any people perceived as outsiders, has already been mentioned. The invention of the printing press in 1440 enabled the mass production of literature, which very quickly came to include pamphlets describing witch trials in lurid detail with accompanying illustrations. Along with such popular literature came treatises debating the reality of witchcraft to and fro. All this served to imprint the image of the satanic witch deeply upon the European imagination.

In 1486, a German Dominican and inquisitor, Heinrich Kramer, published his notorious *Malleus Maleficarum*, or *Hammer of Witches*. The name of a colleague of his, Jakob Sprenger, was later added to the title page, but the work seems to have been Kramer's alone. This book became one of the most influential early printed books, running into 14 editions by 1520. In it, Kramer described the powers and rituals of witchcraft and recommended wiping out all witches by a merciless process of discovery, trial and execution. He claimed that most witches were female because women were essentially inferior to men, being more stupid, greedy and carnal.

MALLEVS
MALEFICARVM,
MALEFICAS ET EARVM
hæresim frameâ conterens,

EX VARIIS AVCTORIBVS COMPILATVS,
& in quatuor Tomos iustè distributus,

QVORVM DVO PRIORES VANAS DÆMONVM versutias, præstigiosas eorum delusiones, superstitiosas Strigimagarum cæremonias, horrendos etiam cum illis congressus; exactam denique tam pestiferæ sectæ disquisitionem, & punitionem complectuntur. Tertius praxim Exorcistarum ad Dæmonum, & Strigimagarum maleficia de Christi fidelibus pellenda; Quartus verò Artem Doctrinalem, Benedictionalem, & Exorcismalem continent.

TOMVS PRIMVS.
Indices Auctorum, capitum, rerúmque non desunt.

Editio nouissima, infinitis penè mendis expurgata; cuique accessit Fuga Dæmonum & Complementum artis exorcisticæ.

Vir siue mulier, in quibus Pythonicus, vel diuinationis fuerit spiritus, morte moriatur Leuitici cap. 10.

LVGDVNI,
Sumptibus CLAVDII BOVRGEAT, sub signo Mercurij Galli.

M. DC. LXIX.
CVM PRIVILEGIO REGIS.

Malleus Maleficarum *or* The Hammer of Witches, *authored by Dominican Heinrich Kramer, is the most influential book promoting the real existence of the witchcraft heresy.*

Nothing that he said was new, but the work served to set out formally the practices of witchcraft together with suggested legal punishments.

Kramer is a problematic figure: misogynistic, corrupt and obsessive. The Dominican Order condemned him in 1490, and Sprenger parted ways with him; however, neither event impeded the influence of the *Malleus* in forming and solidifying the public's image of the witch.

The outlook of the *Canon Episcopi*, which, as described earlier, stated witchcraft to be a delusion, had long been abandoned. Witchcraft was now seen as a satanic plot to destroy the Church; it was the worst of heresies. As such, it attracted increasingly severe legal treatment. During the mediaeval period, the Church left it to individual bishops to investigate dissent.

Each bishop would set up his own inquisition, or formal court of investigation. Between 1227 and 1235, the papal Inquisition was established, and by 1252 it had claimed the right to seize heretics'

Templar Knight following a fleeing enemy, from a fresco in La Chapelle de Cressac, 12th century. The Templar order was founded circa 1119 and disbanded 1314.

Once the authorities
started seeking out
witches rather than
simply waiting for
accusations to roll in, the
witch craze had begun.

goods and to imprison, torture and execute them on slender evidence. The same applied to those accused of witchcraft. Once the authorities started seeking out witches rather than simply waiting for accusations to roll in, the witch craze had begun. The idea that only old, eccentric women were accused is a fallacy. At first the accused included many educated people, including clergymen. Not even the highest in the Church were safe; bishops in both France and England were accused of witchcraft, and Pope Boniface VIII (d.1303) was posthumously accused of signing a pact with the Devil to bring down the Church. As time passed, increasing numbers of ordinary people were drawn into the net, but witchcraft remained a useful charge for ruining influential rivals or enemies. Sometimes the motive was blatant, as in the case of the Knights Templars. This Order had become immensely rich over time, and acted as bankers for several kings across Europe, presenting an irresistible target for those monarchs who were in debt to the Templars. Pope Clement V, Philip IV of France and Edward II of England joined forces to accuse the Templars of making a pact with the Devil, and worshipping him. Scores of Templars were arrested, tortured and executed. Philip IV seized their treasury and demolished their banking system. The Order was suppressed in 1312.

 Burning at the stake was the unlucky fate of most who were caught in the trap of the witch craze.

Surviving witch-trial records can make it seem as if the accused poured forth their confessions voluntarily. However, this impression is highly misleading. Confessions were extracted by a series of questions and, as time passed, lists of standard questions were compiled for the use of inquisitorial courts. Such lists put words into the mouths of the accused, who were given no chance to deny that they'd ever practiced diabolical witchcraft. Instead, they were trapped into answering questions such as:

> *How long have you been a witch? Why did you become a witch?...What was the name of your master among the evil demons?...Where did you consummate your union with your incubus?...What injury have you done to such and such a person, and how did you do it?... How are you able to fly through the air?*

With such leading questions reinforced by torture such as thumbscrews and the strappado, confession became a matter of satisfying the judges in order to stop the agony – even if it led to burning at the stake. Thus a vicious circle was set in motion, each answer reinforcing the beliefs of the accusers and validating the question for further use in later trials. A clerk of the court would be responsible for writing up the process of question-and-answer to make a smooth statement that appeared spontaneous. This should be borne in mind when reading accounts of witch trials.

The possibility of false memory syndrome must also be taken into account when looking at the testimony of the thousands accused of witchcraft. Close questioning can prompt an individual not only to invent occurrences (such as meeting the Devil) but also to actually believe them. The

syndrome only came to light in the 20th century, as psychotherapists began to realize that clients' vivid memories did not necessarily mean that the incident had really happened. The psychological pressure of the trial might well have led some to believe their own confessions. The combination of questioning and recording, the effects of intimidation and torture, meant that what appears in the witch-trial records bears little resemblance to what must truly have taken place. All we can do is read between the lines, with compassion for the accused.

Devils in Loudun

One of the witchcraft trials in Europe has become so notorious as to have a kind of afterlife. The case of the possessed nuns at Loudun has inspired a novel, an opera, a play and a controversial film. The events were unusual in several ways, and still have the power to grip the imagination.

Loudun was a walled city, but Louis XIII felt that any town that could defend itself was a threat to the monarchy and ordered the walls to be demolished. The issue divided the citizens, and tension was ratcheted up further when an outbreak of plague in 1632 killed many inhabitants. In the midst of this unfavourable atmosphere lived the parish priest, Urbain Grandier (1590–1634). He was a strong personality and an ambitious man who was rash enough to make enemies. Not only did he stand against the king's desire to knock down the town walls, he also appeared to sleep

around rather freely with women from rich and powerful families. He balanced his sins with the virtue of being an excellent preacher, but that talent incurred the envy of local monks. Grandier had already had a brush with the law when the possessions began, which was shortly after the plague began to lose its grip.

The nuns at the Ursuline convent had isolated themselves during the plague. Now they began to claim that they had visions of the dead, and that demons were committing all kinds of indecent acts with them. Such sensational claims attracted considerable attention, which seemed to inspire the nuns further. They began to exhibit every sign of demonic possession: blaspheming, exposing themselves, and throwing fits that contorted their bodies in terrifying ways. As they cast around for someone to blame for this supernatural wreckage of their holy peace, they finally lit upon Grandier. He was not their confessor; they did not know him. But his reputation as an attractive libertine must have reached inside the convent walls. Despite Grandier's best efforts to defend himself, the nuns had given his enemies the perfect excuse to try him for witchcraft. They wasted no time.

Grandier was tortured horribly to extort a confession of witchcraft from him: his lower legs were repeatedly squeezed by wooden wedges driven into confining struts until the limbs were reduced to little more than bloody pulp. But this vain and libidinous man suddenly showed his strength of character, insisting to the end on his innocence. It appears that his sufferings were so shocking that some of the nuns publicly recanted, but that did not help Grandier. His supposed pact with the Devil was produced signed by Beelzebub and other demons; a ridiculous stage prop, but one that had the desired effect.

They began to exhibit every sign of demonic possession: blaspheming, exposing themselves, and throwing fits that contorted their bodies in terrifying ways. As they cast around for someone to blame for this supernatural wreckage of their holy peace, they finally lit upon Grandier. He was not their confessor; they did not know him.

The nuns of the convent of Saint-Ursule develop "convent hysteria" and claim to be possessed by demons.

Priest Urbain Grandier is tortured and cruelly burnt on the basis of accusations of licentious behaviour by the hysterical nuns.

So vicious was the hatred of his enemies that Grandier was denied the minor clemency of dying by strangulation before his body was burned: he went alive into the flames. As he died, a flock of pigeons took to the air, which spectators variously interpreted as demons taking his soul to hell or angels mercifully flying him to heaven.

But the nuns, used to being the centre of attention, continued to act as if possessed. The cruel farce of Grandier's trial and death had solved nothing. Three more years passed before the nuns decided they had drained every possible drop of attention from their exploits, and declared that the final demon had been exorcised.

Voices of Reason

The affair of Loudun highlights the blend of hysteria, personal grudges and political expediency that drove the witch trials. Of course, there were a few voices of common sense raised in defence of those accused above those baying for their execution – or silenced by terror. Learned debate was possible up to a point; that point being the publication of *Malleus Maleficarum*, after which those who were sceptical about the existence of satanic witchcraft rarely received a hearing. Henry Cornelius Agrippa (1486–1535) could be said to have inside knowledge since he was known as the foremost occult philosopher of his day. As a real magician, he was well aware that no such beast as a satanic witch existed. Never one to shy away from controversy, he was willing to put

his own life in danger to defend a woman when he saw that justice was not going to be done. The inquisitor for the German town of Metz, where Agrippa lived and worked as an advocate, was a Dominican called Nicholas Savin. Like Kramer, he was known for his harsh treatment of witches. When a peasant woman from a nearby village was accused of witchcraft, her neighbours bribed Savin and his assistant judge, John Leonard, with money and gifts of food. Under such circumstances, a fair trial was not about to happen, and when Agrippa raised his voice in complaint he was removed from the courtroom.

Savin then took the woman back to her village of Vuoypy, where he and Leonard carried on hearing the case even though the village fell outside Leonard's jurisdiction. They had the woman tortured so horribly that the other court officials fled in horror – but that left the woman utterly at Savin's mercy. She was tortured again and left without food or water, seemingly for Savin's sadistic pleasure.

At this point, fate appeared to intervene and Leonard fell seriously ill. On his deathbed, Leonard had a change of heart, regretting his involvement and starting to believe in the woman's innocence. He wrote to Savin, but to no avail. However, after his death, Agrippa took up the cause once again and sent the new judge who replaced Leonard a devastating critique of Savin's brutality. His intervention worked; the woman was freed and her neighbours fined, while Savin was disgraced.

That sounds like a happy ending for the alleged witch, but was it? An anecdote from Scotland in 1678 highlights the problems faced by those who had been accused of evil witchcraft or maleficium. Sir George Mackenzie, a famous lawyer, was shaken when one accused witch told him that she

Heinrich Cornelius Agrippa (1480–1535), German philosopher, diplomat and reputed magician.

Johann Weyer and De praestigiis daemonum.

had confessed to witchcraft not because she was guilty but because "being defam'd for a Witch she knew she would starve…and that all men would beat her, and hound dogs at her, and that therefore she desired to be out of the World; whereupon she wept most bitterly, and upon her knees call'd God to witness what she had said." Nor did Agrippa emerge unscathed from the affair; he had brought such notoriety upon himself that he was forced to flee Metz for Cologne. That was the risk that anyone opposing the persecution of innocent people brought upon themselves.

One of Agrippa's followers, a Dutch physician and occultist called Johann Weyer, bravely published a book in 1563 called *De praestigiis daemonum,* or *On the Tricks of Demons.* He argued that most alleged witchcraft could be explained by perfectly natural means, and that those accused of being witches were suffering from delusions caused by mental problems. For his pains, he was accused of being a witch, although he was not brought to trial.

Weyer's argument influenced Reginald Scot (c.1538–1599) a Member of Parliament and country gentleman. In 1584 he published *The Discoverie of Witchcraft,* in which he used the both Weyer's reasoning and the *Canon Episcopi* to argue that witchcraft was nothing but a delusion. He went on to explain how some feats of magic could be worked, thus ironically providing a wealth of invaluable information that was utilized by cunning folk up until the 19th century.

Even judges who themselves prosecuted witches were not safe from the stake. One example happened in Trier, where one of the worst outbreaks of witch paranoia occurred. A series of trials covering Trier and the surrounding district, held between 1581 and 1593, led to the execution

Johann Weyer argued that most alleged witchcraft could be explained by perfectly natural means, and that those accused of being witches were suffering from delusions caused by mental problems. For his pains, he was accused of being a witch, although he was not brought to trial.

of an unknown number of people; a total of 1,000 has been suggested.

Dietrich Flade, a judge in Trier, was dubious about the use of torture. He conducted witch trials with considerable caution, demanding convincing evidence and doing his best to rein in any signs of unfair persecution. Unfortunately for him, his attitude made him powerful enemies, some of whom were profiting from the confiscated goods of the accused. Flade was accused of plotting to poison the archbishop, and stooges were found to claim they'd seen him at a sabbat (witches' meeting) doing all kinds of vile things. Under torture, he confessed to the point of naming accomplices. He was then strangled and burned. This decent man, who judged according to his conscience, had been pushed by torture far beyond the point of reason, as were thousands of others. All these innocent people contributed, against their will, to the stereotype of the satanic witch.

French philosopher Michel Montaigne (1533–1592) sighed, "It is rating our conjectures too highly to roast people alive for them." Eventually, this balanced and humane view would prevail. But until then, nobody was safe.

Under torture, he confessed to the point of naming accomplices. He was then strangled and burned. This decent man, who judged according to his conscience, had been pushed by torture far beyond the point of reason, as were thousands of others.

SCOT'S
Difcovery of VVitchcraft :
PROVING

The common opinions of Witches con-
tracting with Divels, Spirits, or Familiars; and
their power to kill, torment, and confume the bodies of
men women, and children, or other creatures by difeafes
or otherwife; their flying in the Air, &c. To be but imaginary
Erronious conceptions and novelties;

WHEREIN ALSO,

The lewde unchriftian practifes of Witchmongers, upon aged,
melancholy, ignorant, and fuperftious people in extorting con-
feffions, by inhumane terrors and tortures is notably detected.

ALSO {
The knavery and confederacy of Conjurors.
The impious blafphemy of Inchanters.
The impofture of Soothfayers, and Infidelity of Atheifts.
The delufion of Pythonifts, Figure-cafters, Aftrologers, and va-
nity of Dreamers.
The fruitleffe beggerly art of Alchimiftry.
The horrible art of Poifoning and all the tricks and convey-
ances of juggling and Liegerdemain are fully deciphered.
}

With many other things opened that have long lain hidden: though
very neceffary to be known for the undeceiving of Judges, Juftices,
and Juries, and for the prefervation of poor, aged, deformed, ignorant
people; frequently taken, arraigned, condemned and executed for
Witches, when according to a right underftanding, and a good
confcience, Phyfick, Food, and neceffaries should be
adminiftred to them.

Whereunto is added, a treatife upon the nature, and fubftance of Spirits and Divels,
&c. all written and publifhed in *Anno* 1584. by *Reginald Scot*, Efquire.

LONDON,
Printed by *Richard Cotes.* 1651.

The Discoverie of Witchcraft attempted to bring reason to the subject of the witch trials.

Chapter Four

The Witch on Trial

Three Centuries of Paranoia

THE WITCH-TRIAL CRAZE was an orgy of murderous destruction fuelled by paranoia and personal greed – an orgy that lasted, as noted, for about three centuries. The level of persecution was not standard across either the time period or the geographical area of Europe and the UK. Northern Europe fared particularly badly; there were also comparative lulls in accusations, followed by periods of increasing hysteria.

We now turn our attention to considering the witch trials in depth. Misinformation about the trials is so common that it is worth repeating that the precise number of people legally killed will probably never be known. During the 19th century, wild and unfounded claims were made for figures such as 9 million. Modern Wiccans still talk about the witch craze as the Burning Times and quote such figures. However, as you have learned, the true total probably lies somewhere between 40,000 and 60,000 people who were put to death between 1424 and 1782. That is a horrendous tally of innocent people who were hauled into court, terrified out of their wits, often tortured until their bodies were broken and eventually burned or hanged. In some cases, accusations produced through torture proliferated so widely that entire communities were destroyed.

We already know that the figure of the satanic witch had no basis whatsoever in reality. However, magic was embedded in life and culture, so belief in witchcraft came naturally to most people. Every town and village had its charmers and its cunning men and women. When

misfortune struck, those who were not inclined to accept the Church's explanation that it was God's will might instead look around for a culprit. A victim who suspected witchcraft would visit a cunning person to have the curse removed; this sometimes involved throwing the curse back at the suspected witch so that he or she would suffer the consequences. Other motives, too, might come into play; vengeance could be wreaked on an old enemy by accusing them of witchcraft, or a feared outsider in the community could be removed. Among the higher strata of society, accusations of witchcraft could be used politically.

When the idea of the satanic witch came into the picture, finding and eradicating such enemies of God took on a religious significance behind which those other motives could lurk. And there were even a few warped people, such as Sprenger and Matthew Hopkins, who seemed to relish their deadly work of tormenting and condemning innocent folk.

Both the figure of the witch and the way he or she was treated differed between Britain and Europe. Continental beliefs reflected the old fear of heretical organizations. European witches worked in groups; they flew on pitchforks, shovels, broomsticks or demons in animal shape to regular sabbats, where they ate babies and held sexual orgies. Only rarely did they have familiars – that is, imps in animal form that aided them in their wicked work. Because their essential crime was signing a pact with the Devil, they were accused of heresy and burnt at the stake.

In Britain, witches tended to be solitary, although they were usually accompanied by one or more familiars. Most claimed to have learned their craft from the faeries. In Scotland, witches flew on beanstalks and in sieves; in England,

The witches gather on the Blokula at a Swedish sabbat.

flying witches were rare. They hardly ever attended sabbats, nor were they prone to orgies or cannibalistic feasts. Instead, they contented themselves with working maleficium: causing disease and death to people and livestock, and destroying crops with pests or bad weather. However, as time passed, continental ideas of witchcraft filtered through to Britain, and the image of the witch altered accordingly.

Witchcraft in Britain was a secular crime, the accusation being that of causing harm by maleficium. Torture was not allowed in England, and the sentence was death by hanging; Scottish law differed and condemned the guilty to burn. Some supposed witches were subjected to ordeal by water – that is, being bound and thrown into a pool. If the accused floated, that meant the water rejected them because they were a witch; if they sank, they were innocent. Of course, in the latter case, they might not survive anyway unless they were pulled with alacrity onto dry land. Other ways in which the accused were treated also amounted to mental or physical torture. They might be kept in a room without food or water as the accusers waited for a familiar to appear, or be stripped and searched for a "witch's teat" at which the familiar was supposed to suckle blood. Even worse was the search with a sharp needle for the "witch's mark", supposedly a place on the body that was immune to pain, having been marked by the devil. Any mole or birthmark could be viewed as a witch's mark.

The general activities that witches were thought to pursue were all so unpleasant that it is a wonder nobody ever stopped to ask themselves how likely it was that anyone might want to become a witch. Witches were expected to spend their time doing nothing but ill to their neighbours. In Europe they ate babies and used their bodily fluids for magical ointments; those who attended sabbats had to kiss the Devil's behind, and some who had had sex with the Devil remarked on how painful it was. The accusers were forced to impose on these people the belief that they were totally possessed by evil desires and longings for revenge, rather than according them the usual human motive of the desire for a pleasant (or at least bearable) life. In Europe, the urge to perform witchcraft was seen as the work of the Devil, who never ceased his campaign

Witchcraft in Britain was a secular crime, the accusation being that of causing harm by maleficium. Torture was not allowed in England, and the sentence was death by hanging...

against humankind; in Britain, it implied a warped and profoundly unpleasant personality. The image of the witch was a world away from the beneficent *benandanti*, flying out at night to fight for the good of the community, or the followers of Diana enjoying their nocturnal feasts.

Dame Alice and Her Children

Although in Britain witchcraft was seen as a hate crime rather than as heresy, one very early case proved an exception. Dame Alice Kyteler was a wealthy woman from Kilkenny in Ireland. She outlived three husbands, and when her fourth fell ill he suspected she was poisoning him with powders found amongst her possessions. Dame Alice's children from her earlier marriages then accused her of using witchcraft to kill her previous husbands, thus depriving the children of their inheritance. In 1324, they accused her of being a 'heretic sorcerer', and in no time the Bishop of Ossory had charged 11 other people with being her accomplices, including her maid, Petronilla de Meath, and her favourite son, William Outlaw.

Dame Alice and her accomplices were said to have renounced Christ. They met at night, at a lonely crossroads, where they offered a rather exotic sacrifice of nine red cocks and nine peacocks' eyes to a demon called Robert Artisson. He appeared as a black cat or dog, or in human

 Street art on St Kieran Street in Kilkenny of Dame Alice Kyteler by Mick Minogue.

form, also black. Two tall men armed with iron rods accompanied him. When he was in human form, Dame Alice would have sex with him. Robert taught the group witchcraft, including the use of ointments made with dead men's fingernails and the shrouds of unbaptized babies, stirred in a cauldron made from the skull of an executed criminal. Sometimes they would indulge in orgies.

Quite apart from these standard activities that were usually practised in Europe, Dame Alice went out every night to sweep the streets of Kilkenny, not from a sense of civic duty, but to work a charm. By morning all the dirt would have been heaped up outside her son William's front door; an undesirable result, but one that magically brought him riches.

Dame Alice was simply allowed to escape, whereupon she fled to England and stirred up trouble against the accusing Bishop, who was himself accused of heresy and disgraced. Alice's son William was imprisoned, but won his freedom by promising to re-roof Kilkenny cathedral. Those without power were not so lucky; Alice's maid Petronilla refused to recant and, after being flogged repeatedly, was burned at the stake. The case of Dame Alice still mystifies because it so uncannily foreshadows much later developments.

The Devil Shapeshifts

Since in Britain witchcraft was a secular offence, laws were passed against it in order to clarify exactly what counted as acts of maleficium. The first

such act was passed in 1542 under Henry VIII, but it was so rarely used that it was repealed in 1547. The law forbade the use of sorcery to cast love charms or cause harm, or to find treasure buried under old stone crosses; apparently many of these had been destroyed in such futile searches. All three activities would commonly have been performed not by witches, but by cunning folk, but then the line between the two was never clearly drawn and some cunning folk (though fewer than might be expected) suffered the fate of the witch.

In 1563 another law was passed under Elizabeth I, the penalty this time being reduced to a year in prison for a first offence, though a relapse incurred a death sentence. The first notable trial using this act occurred in 1566 in Chelmsford, Essex – a county that was to suffer disproportionately during the witch-trial craze.

This trial of three women shows the differences between European and British witch activity, and sets a template for trials to come. To begin with the women – Elizabeth Francis, Agnes Waterhouse and her daughter Joan – were accused of various acts of maleficium, including the bewitchment of a child. The records do not reveal all the means that were used to make the women confess, but we have already found that ill treatment could have included solitary confinement and being left without food or drink. We know that both Elizabeth and Agnes were shaved, stripped and pricked, because the trial records note that blemishes were found on their bodies. Perhaps that humiliating and painful experience was enough to inspire Elizabeth to feel she had not confessed enough, and she expanded on her life as a witch. Simply being in court, facing men of authority and from a higher class, must have been intimidating enough. We should remember at this

The hanging of three witches is depicted in a woodcut from an English pamphlet of 1569.

point that although trial records are written so that a confession appears as a spontaneously offered continuous narrative, what it really represents is a series of answers to leading questions.

The procedure of questioning the accused was standard in all criminal cases. The right set of questions could lead the accused to incriminate him or herself; we have already looked at some of these in Chapter Three. Even when court records note that a confession was made voluntarily, that was not at all the case. None of the accused are ever likely to have stood up in

court and poured out a tale of their evil doings, no matter how the records were manipulated to make it appear that they did.

Elizabeth Francis claimed that she had learned witchcraft as a child from her grandmother, who gave her a familiar in the form of a cat named Sathan, which was in fact the Devil. Sathan could speak, and required feeding not only with bread and milk but also Elizabeth's blood, as was traditional with familiars. But even with Sathan's assistance, things did not go well for Elizabeth. Her lover abandoned her, leaving her with an

✠ *A cat Sathan, or Satan, who figured as a witch familiar in the Chelmsford trials of 1579. From a contemporaneous tract dealing with the Trials.*

unwanted pregnancy. Sathan, however, taught her how to bring about an abortion. Elizabeth later married and had a daughter, but she did not take to the child, and Sathan dispatched it for her.

Perhaps Elizabeth felt she had had enough of demonic help, because after 16 years she gave Sathan to Agnes Waterhouse in return for a cake. Agnes tested Sathan's powers by making him kill one of her own pigs, but after quarrelling with her neighbours she let him loose on their geese and cattle. Like Elizabeth, Agnes fed Sathan with her blood and kept him in a box lined with wool. When she decided that she wanted to use the wool, she persuaded Sathan to turn himself into a toad.

Agnes' daughter Joan also made use of Sathan when a neighbour's young daughter refused her a piece of bread and cheese. According to the child, Agnes sent Sathan to her in the form of a large black dog with horns and an ape's face that stole the key to the dairy and ate the butter there. This unflappable child did not run screaming from the monster, but calmly asked who his owner was, at which he nodded his head towards Agnes' house. While Joan admitted that Sathan took a dog's form when he worked for her, she claimed he certainly didn't look like an ape, and therefore cannot have been the creature that had tormented the child. Rather surprisingly, she was found not guilty. Neither Agnes nor Elizabeth was so lucky, but only Agnes was given the death sentence. However, 13 years later Elizabeth was accused again of witchcraft, and this time she, too, was hanged.

This sorry affair is notable for the domestic details of the women's lives, so very different from the melodramatic pact-signings and orgiastic sabbats of the European witch trials. It tells of petty quarrels and of hunger – hunger that can be appeased with a simple piece of bread and cheese rather than feasting on dead babies at the Devil's table. And yet, the result was the same: the death penalty, and for survivors a ruined reputation and hostile, suspicious neighbours.

As the idea took hold that any unfortunate incident could be blamed not on bad luck but on witchcraft, the witch-trial craze gathered momentum. The victims were mostly women, variously accused of causing sickness, killing chickens, making cows give blood instead of milk, ruining crops and indeed being responsible for any of the disasters of everyday life.

During the 1580s – the worst period – the number of cases accounted for about 13 per cent of all criminal trials. Not all cases ended in execution. Witchcraft was a difficult crime to prove, and some judges may have harboured private doubts about its existence, so the acquittal rate was high. However, as previously mentioned, there was no guarantee that those who were able to return to their communities would be welcomed there. Some, like Elizabeth Francis, were watched with suspicion and accused again.

The Trial of Ursula Kemp

She continued to help her neighbours with cures, until events turned against her. One of her accusers, Grace Thurlow, recounted that although Ursula used the lameness cure successfully on her, she had been unable to pay the 12 pence demanded… her son then fell ill, and when he began to recover, Grace's former lameness returned.

One trial in particular stands out during this period, partly because the obvious injustice of the accusations and punishment inspired Reginald Scot to write his refutation of witchcraft, *The Discoverie of Witchcraft*. The trial took place in Essex early in 1582, with Justice of the Peace Brian Darcy of St. Osyth presiding. The accusations demonstrate how precarious the lives of cunning men and women had become during this period of witchcraft paranoia.

According to Ursula Kemp, she had been unwell with a "lameness in her bones" some ten years previously, and had consulted a cunning woman. She was told that she had been bewitched, and was given instructions for a curative ritual. This is interesting as an example of traditional cunning, utilizing magic, psychology and herb-craft. Ursula had to:

> *Take hogs' dung and charcoal and put them together and hold them in her left hand, and to take in the other hand a knife, and to prick the medicine three times, and then to cast the same into a fire, and to take the said knife and make three pricks under a table, and to let the knife stick there. And after that to take three leaves of sage, and as much of herb John…and put them into ale, and drink it last at night and first in the morning…*

The cure worked, and Ursula subsequently used it to cure two other women who were suffering from a similar illness. She continued to help her neighbours with cures, until events turned against her. One of her accusers, Grace Thurlow, recounted that although Ursula used the lameness cure successfully on her, she had been unable to pay the 12 pence demanded and had refused when Ursula asked for some cheese instead. Her son then fell ill, and when he began to recover, Grace's former lameness returned. Even though Ursula had specifically said to her that 'though she could unwitch she could not witch', Grace believed that Ursula was responsible for her suffering.

The second witness was Annis Letherdall, who told the court that Ursula had requested some scouring sand, offering to dye a pair of women's hose in return. Annis had refused, giving Ursula's bad reputation as an excuse. When Annis' daughter fell ill, she accused Ursula of witchcraft. Ursula denied bewitching the child, but to no avail.

The bones of Ursula Kemp, the witch of St Osyth in Essex, who was executed in Chelmsford in 1589, are exhibited in Boscastle Witches Museum, Cornwall.

Perhaps the most shocking aspect of this affair was that Ursula's own son Thomas 'of the age of 8 years or thereabouts', informed on her. The child would doubtless have been thoroughly scared by the proceedings, and since there is no record of what questions were asked him, we have no way of assessing how much of his testimony was suggested to him. Thomas claimed that his mother had not just one familiar imp, but four, which she nourished with beer and her own blood: '…Tittey is like a little grey cat, Tyffin is like a white lamb, Pigeon is black like a toad, and Jack is black like a cat.' During her confession to Brian Darcy, Ursula confirmed that

The Cage, a mediaeval prison in St. Osyth. Ursula Kemp was imprisoned here before being hanged as a witch in 1582. It was last used as a prison in 1908.

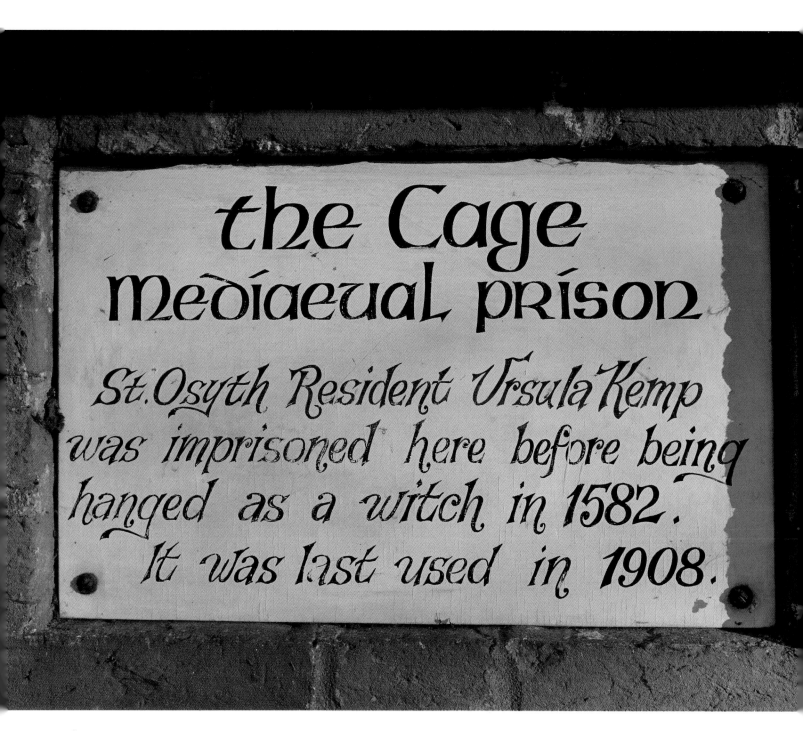

A sign at the prison commemorating Ursula Kemp and her imprisonment in the Cage.

she owned these rather charming pets, although once again it is impossible to say how the questions to her were framed – they could have been along the lines of, "Do you have a familiar called Tittey? Does it appear like a grey cat?"

Darcy promised Ursula leniency if she cooperated, at which she fell on her knees weeping, clearly in deep distress. A confession was obtained from her of various acts of witchcraft including magical murder. Ursula named 12 other women as fellow witches. But Darcy reneged on his promise, and at least one of those women was hanged, along with poor Ursula, in 1582. At least four women died in prison, and one was only released as late as 1588.

The St. Osyth trials show clearly how even the best-intentioned person could fall foul of the law – and then, how the accusations could ripple outwards. In this case women from at least six other villages found themselves hauled into court. Everyone for miles around must have been on edge, and keeping an eye out for suspicious behaviour.

Witches Against the King

Into this already poisonous atmosphere was now brought the influence of a new king, who was terrified of witches. James VI of Scotland had probably imbibed ideas about continental witchcraft from his connection with Denmark, from whose royal family his bride came. When

Anne of Denmark set off to join her fiancé in Scotland, storms forced her ship in to Norway. In a rare moment of romance, James set sail to collect her and brought her safely home. However, rumours circulated about the storm – had it been brewed up by witches? The admiral of the Danish fleet thought so, and a witch trial ensued in Copenhagen that resulted in the execution of two women.

James heard about this trial and must have decided that the Danish witches were in league with Scottish colleagues. His involvement led to a trial that was unusual in its resemblance to the European witch trials. Indeed, the affair of the Berwick witches in 1590-1592 became one of the most notorious witch trials in history. As with the downfall of Ursula Kemp, it began with a seemingly benevolent activity.

Gilly Duncan, a young servant from North Berwick, suddenly developed healing powers and began to leave her place of employment during the night to help her neighbours as a charmer or cunning person. But her employer, a magistrate called David Seton, grew suspicious and decided to question her about her abilities. He was known as a fervent witch hunter, and he blamed his financial troubles on witchcraft. Gilly was unforthcoming until Seton set about torturing her. He used pilliwinks (a misleadingly playful name for an instrument similar to thumbscrews) and a wet rope twisted around her head. Eventually Gilly confessed and was passed to the authorities for prosecution. Threatened with more torture, she began naming others, including citizens of good standing such as Agnes Simpson, an elderly and well-educated lady, and Dr. John Fian, a schoolmaster.

King James I of England (and VI of Scotland) (1566–1625) and his wife, Anne of Denmark (1574–1619).

The North Berwick Witches: engraving showing Satan luring Dr Fian and other misguided people to indulge in evil practices such as causing shipwrecks by casting spells.

North Berwick Witches and Dr Fian depicted in flight within a churchyard.

Scottish law allowed torture to be used, and both people suffered horribly. Agnes was deprived of sleep while wearing a witch's bridle, an iron contraption with sharp prongs that pressed against the tongue and cheeks. Dr. Fian had his fingernails pulled out and iron pins thrust into his fingertips; he suffered the pilliwinks and the boot (the device that crushed Urbain Grandier's legs). Under such agonizing treatment it is hardly surprising that both confessed to the charges laid against them. They were said to have sailed in a great company of witches, all in sieves, to North Berwick church on Halloween. Black candles illuminated the church, and there they met the Devil, whose buttocks they kissed in true continental fashion. The witches had planned to kill the king by raising a storm to sink his ship and, if that failed, Agnes was to employ a charm using toads' blood to the same end.

Newes from Scotland,
Declaring the Damna-
ble life and death of Doctor Fian, *a*
notable Sorcerer, who was burned at
Edenbrough in Ianuary laſt.
1591.

Which Doctor was regeſter to the Diuell
that ſundry times preached at North Bar-
rick Kirke, to a number of notorious Witches.

With the true examinations of the ſaide Doctor
and Witches, as they vttered them in the pre-
ſence of the Scottiſh King.

Diſcouering how they pretended
to bewitch and drowne his Maieſtie in the Sea
comming from Denmarke, with ſuch
*other wonderfull matters as the like
hath not been heard of at
any time.*

Publiſhed according to the Scottiſh Coppie.

AT LONDON
Printed for William
Wright.

The North Berwick Witches are denounced, along with Dr Fian. Title page of a book printed on the orders of King James VI of Scotland (probably written by James Carmichael), which features the Scottish witchcraft case.

The king himself was present at some of the trials, which must have been an extra source of intimidation for the accused. Dr. Fian was executed in Edinburgh by strangulation followed by the burning of the body on 27th January 1591, and Agnes Sampson met the same fate the following day. Edinburgh Treasury records note the cost of materials for both executions: £5 18s 2d for Dr. Fian, and for Agnes, £5 8s 10d.

In 1603, James VI of Scotland ascended to the English throne as James I. He had already published an attack on the sceptical views of Reginald Scot and Johann Weyer in his *Daemonologie* (1597), which included an account of the Berwick witches. But refuting Scot's views was not enough for the king; once ensconced on the English throne, James ordered all copies of

But refuting Scot's views was not enough for the king; once ensconced on the English throne, James ordered all copies of Scot's book to be burned.

Scot's book to be publicly burned. Thus the book suffered the same fate as many Scottish witches.

Parliament passed a new law against witchcraft in 1604 that was considerably harsher than the 1563 law. First offences of causing harm by witchcraft or exhuming a corpse for magical purposes now incurred the death penalty, and divining for hidden treasure was punishable by a life sentence.

James I is remembered with respect for commissioning a new translation of the Bible in the same year that the witchcraft law was passed, 1604. The King James Bible was published in 1611, and is justly celebrated both for the beauty of its language and the enduring and profound influence it has exerted on British literature and culture. However, there is a dark side to the Bible. The famous phrase from Exodus 22:18, 'Thou shalt not suffer a witch to live,' is in fact a mistranslation that may have been made in order to please the witch-fearing king. The original Hebrew term translated as 'witch' is *mekhashepha*, which has been variously interpreted to mean poisoner or herbalist. However, the Biblical phrase gave divine sanction to the pursuit and execution of those perceived as practising witchcraft, and it is still quoted today.

As time passed, even the terror-ridden King began to see reason and revise his views on witchcraft. By 1616, he was having doubts serious enough for him to halt a trial being held in Leicester, through which he happened to be passing at the time. James himself questioned the main prosecution witness, a twelve-year-old boy, and pronounced him a liar. Nine witches had already been hanged on the boy's word, and another six languished in prison awaiting trial. James had them freed and reprimanded the judge for his gullibility.

Witch Families
of Pendle

But James' change of heart came too late to help many, including those hanged as a result of the famous Pendle witch trial in 1612, during which accusations proliferated until 21 people had been convicted. This was the first large trial since the 1604 law had been passed, and once again the result depended on the testimony of a child. It has become one of the best-known English witch trials because of the unusually large pamphlet of 188 pages that described the proceedings in detail. Witch trials were a publisher's dream; sensational, titillating and horrifying, they were just what the public wanted.

The first people to be accused were two old women known as Old Demdike and Old Chattox. Old Demdike's real name was Elizabeth Southern; rumours that she was a witch had circulated for a long time before her arrest. Her neighbour, Ann Whittle, was given the nickname Old Chattox because of her habit of muttering to herself – a dangerous habit, since she might be whispering curses. Under questioning, Old Demdike claimed that she had been recruited by the Devil in the shape of a boy 52 years previously; she and Old Chattox were aided in their wicked work of murder and conspiracy by their daughters and sundry relatives and neighbours.

Old Demdike's granddaughter, Alison Device, confessed to cursing an itinerant peddler when he refused to give her pins for free. He then appears to have suffered a stroke that twisted his face and paralyzed his limbs. Old Chattox was accused of bewitching one Robert Nutter to death, aided by Old Demdike's daughter, Elizabeth Device, and her own daughter, Anne Redfearne. Old Demdike, Old Chattox and Alison Device were imprisoned in Lancaster Castle, there to await the August Assizes.

The story now takes what would have been an almost farcical turn had it not ended so tragically. Early in April, Elizabeth Device called a meeting of the two families at her mother's home in order to discuss getting the women out of jail. About 20 men and women attended, plotting over a large meal of beef, bacon and stolen mutton (and probably much alcohol). They agreed to kill the jailer, blow up the castle and whisk the prisoners away.

This unlikely plot was leaked, leading to the arrest and imprisonment of those family members who failed to flee in time. One by one they all began to accuse each other, and their testimony shows that Continental ideas of witchcraft were now seeping into British culture. The witches were said to fly to sabbats on broomsticks, and they fed drops of their own blood to their familiars in order to seal the satanic pact they had made.

The evidence given by Elizabeth Device and her children James (who was in his early twenties) and Jannet (aged nine) secured the convictions that took ten people to the gallows. The young people also accused their own mother, claiming that she kept a familiar spirit like a brown dog called Ball. This entity helped her commit murder, and she also used clay figurines (known as poppets) to work her evil. Jannet then turned on her brother, but her imagination failed her at this point and she stated that he, too, had a dog-familiar named Dandy that he also used to bewitch people to death.

Mother Chattox with two of the supposed victims of her sorcery.

Witches on broomsticks ride through the night sky.

Elizabeth, too, made a confession, but she later retracted it. Others among the accused vehemently asserted their innocence, and even the judge harboured doubts about the value of the evidence, some of which relied on very old gossip. When a wealthy land-owning woman, Alice Nutter, was drawn into the circle of the accused, solely on the word of James, Jannet and Elizabeth, Judge Bromley evidently suspected that Jannet knew her only by name and had accused her at random. He had Dame Nutter brought into court among a group of women, but she was a well-known figure locally and Jannet passed this test with flying colours.

Despite the retractions and the flimsy evidence, ten of the accused were hanged, including the hapless Alice Nutter, Old Chattox and her daughter Ann Redfearne, Elizabeth Device, her son James and her eleven-year-old daughter Alison. Old Demdike died in jail. Two others were sentenced to a year in jail, with four sessions in the pillory.

The trial of the Pendle witches – clearly a massive miscarriage of justice – has resonated through the centuries, inspiring books, songs and films. The witches have been claimed as counter-cultural heroes and heroines, and the area of Pendle Hill has embraced them as a tourist gimmick, with witch dolls, a statue of Alice Nutter, a Witches Brew beer and sundry other offerings. The fourth centenary of the trial in 2012 was marked by a series of events and commissions, including a commemorative poem written by Carol Ann Duffy that is engraved on stones along a 51-mile trail leading from Pendle Hill to Lancaster Castle.

In 1634, the tables were turned on Jannet Device when she in her turn was accused of

The trial of the Pendle witches – clearly a massive miscarriage of justice – has resonated through the centuries, inspiring books, songs and films.

witchcraft along with about 30 other people. The affair became known as the Pendle Swindle and, as in the previous trial, a child's evidence was taken as gospel truth. The child in this case was Edmund Robinson, the son of a local farmer. He seems to have invented a wild story to escape punishment for failing to look after his father's cattle. Edmund claimed that he had come across two greyhounds, which he appropriated and set on a hare. When the dogs refused the chase, he started to hit them, upon which they turned into a young boy and a neighbour called Mother Dickenson. They tried to persuade Edmund to join them in serving the Devil, but he refused. The boy then turned into a horse, and Mother Dickenson grabbed Edmund, pulling him with her onto the horse's back. Off they flew to a barn, where a sabbat was being celebrated. As so often happens in witch trials, food was the focus, and Edmund watched as a wonderful feast was lowered on ropes from the ceiling. Refusing temptation, Edmund escaped, though not before committing to memory the faces of all 50 people present.

Edmund's father made sure that he told his story to the local authorities, who unwisely promised to pay him a sum for every witch he could identify. Edmund started to travel round the local villages, and soon 30 people had been accused. At this point, the Bishop of Chester was asked to investigate. Clearly more astute than the local authorities, the Bishop soon uncovered evidence that Edmund's father was working a protection racket, taking money from locals to ensure Edmund passed them over. He was jailed. However, it seems that not all of the accused were immediately freed, for records show that Jannet Device was still imprisoned two long years later.

Witchfinder General

The early 17th century was a time of great political and religious tension in Britain. Parliament rose up against King Charles I, leading to the English Civil War that tore the country apart from 1642 to 1651. Charles was captured in 1648, accused of treason and sentenced to death. He was beheaded in January 1649, and the turbulent period of the Commonwealth under Oliver Cromwell followed. Peace and stability were restored only with the triumphant return from exile of Charles' son, Charles II, in 1666.

Into the atmosphere of fear and suspicion generated by war stepped Matthew Hopkins, undoubtedly the most notorious person associated with English witchcraft. His name has become synonymous with cruelty for a good reason; in less than two years he caused more people to be hanged for witchcraft in England than in the previous century.

Hopkins was an unremarkable man until he reinvented himself. He came from Suffolk and his father was a puritan minister. He studied law but without marked success; in fact, he was unable to make a living in Ipswich and moved to Manningtree in Essex to make a fresh start. Eastern England was a hotbed of Puritans, hence tensions ran particularly high there. In such an atmosphere, a ruthless man could easily point out scapegoats for any kind of trouble, and that is what Hopkins did. Cannily avoiding the political minefield, he read James I's *Daemonologie* and aimed his malice at the poor and ignorant, accusing them of conspiratorial satanic witchcraft in the European style.

Matthew Hopkins, the Witchfinder General.

Elizabeth also claimed during the period of her torture that the Devil had regularly visited her for sex, appearing in her bedroom three or four times a week over the past six or seven years and murmuring 'Bessie, I must lie with you.' The sexual fantasy of a poor, disabled, and doubless lonely, woman was taken as gospel truth.

Hopkins claimed that he held a commission from parliament, although that has never been proved, and set himself up as Witchfinder General. Although Hopkins' assumption of this title suggests that there were other witchfinders in the country, that was not the case; he appears to have been the only person who discovered how to turn the hunting of witches into a lucrative career.

Hopkins found an associate, John Stearne, and assembled a band of assistants that, rather shockingly, included at least one woman, Mary Phillips. He began his campaign in 1644 in his own town of Manningtree by making an accusation of witchcraft against an elderly and disabled woman, Elizabeth Clarke. Hopkins claimed that he had overheard her and her associates talking about their meetings with the Devil. Her confession was obtained by keeping her without sleep for four days; one of Hopkins' unpleasant talents was his inventive use of torture that could not be named as such because it left no mark upon the body.

Elizabeth also claimed during the period of torture that the Devil had regularly visited her for sex, appearing in her bedroom three or four times a week over the past six or seven years and murmuring, "Bessie, I must lie with you." The sexual fantasy of a poor, disabled and doubtless lonely woman was taken as gospel truth. Elizabeth also offered to show Hopkins and his cohort one of her familiar imps, which Hopkins refused in righteous horror. Nevertheless, both he and his assistants claimed that four familiars made brief appearances as a white dog, a greyhound, a polecat and a black imp.

Under duress, Elizabeth soon named other witches, and the circle of accusations rippled outwards until 23 women had been accused. They were tried in Chelmsford in 1645. The numbers recorded are unclear but it seems that 19 were hanged while some had already died in prison and others were still imprisoned four years later. Some women were condemned to the gallows merely for keeping a pet. One such person was Bridget Mayers, a sailor's wife, who was accused of entertaining an imp in the shape of a mouse she called "Prick-ears".

Hopkins and his crew did not wait for the conclusion of the trials. Flushed with their success, they set off on their witch-finding travels around Essex, Suffolk and Norfolk. Everywhere they went, they employed the various means of torture available to them, such as pricking, swimming, isolation, and sleep deprivation. Victims were bound and made to sit cross-legged for long periods of time, or walked up and down until their feet bled – all without sleep or nourishment. Such techniques did not count as torture, but neither did they make Hopkins popular.

Hopkins' motives for his vicious and unique campaign have never been properly untangled. He may well have believed his own propaganda and wished to rid the country of Devil-worship – but he also made a tidy profit. The average wage at that time was sixpence per day, but Hopkins received payment in pounds sterling in every town he visited; for example, the authorities in Aldeburgh disbursed £6, and Stowmarket paid an extortionate £23. In one place, Hopkins was said to have demanded that town officials levy a special tax on the inhabitants to raise £28 for him and his assistants. In two years he may have earned as much as £1,000 – a fortune at that time.

Hopkins' campaign swiftly assumed nightmarish proportions. In 1645, at the Suffolk sessions at Bury St. Edmunds, around 200 people were detained under suspicion of witchcraft. Included in their number was a venerable parson, 70-year-old John Lowes. Hopkins' team "ran" him, keeping him moving without sleep for several nights on end, then allowing him to rest briefly before forcing him to walk again. Under this brutal treatment, Lowes finally confessed to signing the traditional pact with the Devil, suckling familiars, bewitching cattle and – a spectacular feat – drowning 14 people by causing a ship to sink off Harwich on a calm day. Such was the irrational fear that Hopkins aroused that nobody even checked whether a ship had in fact sunk when Lowes claimed.

Lowes retracted his confession, but that did him no good. He was not allowed another clergyman to read the burial service over him, so he did it himself as he was taken to the scaffold.

Hopkins continued to crisscross eastern England, sometimes descending on a town more than once. In the four months between September 1645 and January 1646 he visited Aldeburgh in Suffolk no fewer than three times. More than 128 people were arrested for witchcraft in Suffolk, and at least 68 of them were hanged. But by now, thanks to Hopkins' greed and obsessive pursuit of helpless victims, questions were beginning to be asked. A Parliamentary newsletter called *The Moderate Intelligencer* commented that when such large numbers were accused, there should be close investigation into the charges before a death sentence was pronounced.

In 1646, a clergyman called John Gaule began preaching against Hopkins. He published a pamphlet exposing Hopkins' techniques for forcing a confession, proving them to be torture pure and simple. Hopkins responded with another pamphlet, *Discovery of Witches,* claiming he was doing God's work. But the tide had turned against him; he had simply accused too many people and been too avaricious. He was questioned in court about his fees and torture techniques.

Hopkins' career vanished as swiftly as it had arisen. In the summer of 1646 he retired to Manningtree and obscurity. Such was his notoriety that legend has demanded a suitably ironic twist to his tale. The tale was long circulated that Hopkins was himself accused of witchcraft and "swum" – and that he floated, and was condemned. Satisfying though such poetic justice would be, Hopkins died mundanely of tuberculosis, not long after his retirement.

After Hopkins, there were only a few more mass witch trials in England. Records of 1645-1646 are incomplete, so it is impossible to say precisely how many died as a result of Hopkins' campaign, but it is likely to be in the low hundreds. Estimates have suggested that Hopkins was responsible for 20 per cent of all witchcraft executions in the period between the early fifteenth and late 18th centuries – all within a period of about 14 months.

I Shall Go into a Hare

One trial that took place in Scotland has echoed down the centuries just as loudly as the Witchfinder General's exploits, though for very different reasons. In April 1662, a woman called Isobel Gowdie was brought before the authorities in Auldearn, a small village on the edge of the

Highlands. Tradition has it that Isobel voluntarily confessed to being a witch, and legend has turned her into a young, flame-haired beauty. In fact, she was almost certainly accused of witchcraft along with other women and men. There is no record of either her age or what she looked like; all that is known is that she seems to have been the wife of a farmer or labourer.

Under questioning, Isobel made four confessions over a period of six weeks. Although the confessions cover the same material, each one is increasingly detailed. There are some similarities between what Isobel stated and the confessions of other Scottish witches, but her confessions stand out as being remarkable for both their amount of detail and her vivid turn of phrase. Isobel's confessions make for strange reading, jumbling together as they do genuine folk practices along with material in line with the stereotype of satanic witchcraft that the confessors managed to extract from her. This included wild imaginings of demonic attendants and lurid descriptions of sex with the Devil.

Isobel mingled folklore and descriptions of cunning techniques with her tale of being initiated by the Devil, attending sabbats and participating in demonic orgies. She described being entertained by the fairy king and queen under the Downie Hill, and being frightened by the bulls they kept. She gave details of joining other witches to kill the local Laird's children by making a poppet. She claimed to have raised winds, magically stolen fish and cursed the local minister with sickness. She spoke of riding straws to the sabbat and of randomly shooting people with elf-darts as she flew. These elf-darts are the same prehistoric flint arrowheads that Anglo-Saxons believed the elves would shoot to cause sickness,

At her 1662 trial, Scottish witch Isobel Gowdie tells how since 1647 she and her companions were visited by "Black John" who chastised disobedient witches.

so Isobel's confession records an astonishing survival and adaptation of an idea across the centuries. Isobel claimed that she flicked the darts off her thumbnail, and that she had murdered several people that way. They did not die at once, but within a short space of time they would sicken and fail.

Some of Isobel's material has been incorporated into modern Wiccan practice. When she made a pact with the Devil, she was told to put one hand on her head and the other under the sole of one foot whilst she vowed everything in between to him. This ritual is known to be have been used by Scottish seers in order to temporarily give their

> **Isobel named 12 other people with whom she worked; she called the group a coven, and this is the first record of the word...**

that she and her colleagues could shapeshift into animals including jackdaws, crows, cats and hares. Her rhyming charm for turning into a hare and back again has entered modern witchcraft in various versions, the original being somewhat difficult to read and with some words missing.

> *I shall go into a hare,*
> *With sorrow and sigh and mickle care,*
> *And I shall go in the Devil's name,*
> *Aye while I come home again.*
> *(Repeat three times)*
> *(To return to human form)*
> *Hare, hare, God send thee care!*
> *I am in a hare's shape just now,*
> *But I shall be in woman's shape even now.*

After all her vivid and detailed descriptions of cunning and of imagined demonic witchcraft, Isobel dropped out of history as if she had never been. Her fate is unknown; there is no record of whether she was burned as a witch or acquitted and allowed to return quietly home. The historians who have looked in depth at her case mostly agree that she would have been condemned and executed. However, that has not prevented the force of nature that was Isobel from living on in memory. She has been commemorated in folk music, novels, plays, art and lectures.

Isobel has been reimagined as a fiercely independent and romantic woman oppressed by masculine authorities and claimed as an archetype of the feminist theory of witchcraft. Ultimately, she has triumphed – and in so doing, she can be said to have done so for all witches, both female and male, who lived hard lives that were ended brutally, all for the sake of a crazed idea.

ability of second sight to one not thus blessed. Some witch covens today incorporate it into their initiation rituals as a sign of dedication to Wicca.

Isobel named 12 other people with whom she worked; she called the group a coven, and this is the first record of a word that has since passed into common parlance, together with the notion that a traditional coven consists of 13 witches. Isobel's coven had a Maiden who seems to have enjoyed particular favours from the Devil, and Wiccan covens nowadays often appoint a Maiden who takes a prominent role in rituals.

Perhaps most famously, as the confessions continued Isobel began to embroider the by now familiar material with rhymed charms such as would be used by cunning folk. She claimed

From Europe the witch craze made its way to America and the famous Salem witch trials.

Chapter Five

Old Magic,
New Worlds

Magic Before America Was Born

HISTORICALLY SPEAKING, NORTH America is a young country compared with Europe, but humans have lived there since prehistory. While the earliest date of occupation is debated, people were definitely making their homes on the continent from about 11,500 BCE. They had travelled over the Bering Strait land bridge that then existed between the North American continent and Siberia, possibly bringing shamanic practices with them.

The evidence is hard to interpret, but it seems that from about 8,000 BCE, pilgrimages were being made to certain sites considered sacred. At Poverty Point in the lower Mississippi Valley, a large site dating to between 1700 and 1100 BCE has been excavated consisting of man-made mounds and ridges where houses were once built. The area is not stony, yet quantities of stone worked into various forms have been found there. It could be that people brought stone as an offering, taking away some other item in return that they saw as being imbued with some of the sacred quality of the place.

Thus it appears that magical activity in North America is as old as humanity. Shamanism threads through the magical history of the country right up to the present day, although the term is controversial. Some Native Americans feel strongly that it is a cultural appropriation from Siberia and that many of their practices differ from those of traditional Siberian shamans. However, the term "shaman" has by now lost its original precise application. It has become a popular term applied to magical practitioners from any culture, who deal with the spirit world and advise their community accordingly – and it is in this sense that it is used here.

Native American shamans heal the sick and protect the vulnerable against malicious magic. They communicate with the spirits of animals and garner their help. Each shaman has his or her own spirit animal guide or accomplice. Such people are magicians who serve their communities – the opposite of the imaginary witch of Europe and Britain who sought only to harm and destroy.

Native American shamans heal the sick and protect the vulnerable against malicious magic. Such people are magicians who serve their communities.

A Virginian shaman, circa 1720.

Old Witchcraft in the New Colonies

The men and women who sailed to America in 1620 dreamed of starting a new life free from the influence of the Church of England, which they regarded as hopelessly corrupt. Sadly, they brought with them the fantasy of the satanic witch that was causing so much destruction across Europe and Britain. We have already seen that they protected their buildings with so-called witch marks, and they also brought a strong superstitious fear of the Devil's power that was about to wane and die out in Europe. Indeed, the terrible affair of the Salem witches has been called the last flare-up of the witch trials. However, it was not the only trial for witchcraft enacted on American soil, although it was by far the largest, most spectacular and most brutally murderous. The Puritans landed in what was to them a new and totally unknown land, a wilderness already occupied by Native Ameri-

cans. Their settlements must have felt extremely vulnerable, and fears of attack, unknown illness and adverse weather must have run high. Under such conditions, anyone with a reputation for ill humour or unwillingness to share scarce goods would quickly fall under suspicion whenever illness or other disasters struck the community. Almost immediately, courts across the colonies began to try cases of witchcraft. The first that appears in the records occurred in Virginia.

Joan Wright appears to have been a cunning woman and midwife, since she was called upon to help the wife of one Giles Allington through childbirth. However, Mrs. Allington distrusted Joan because she was left-handed, and she involved a Mrs. Gray as well. Unfortunately, both the Allingtons and their newborn child fell ill, and the child died. At this point Mrs. Gray heaped coals on the fire by claiming that Joan had correctly prophesied the death of several neighbours. Joan's reputation for prophesy must already have got

Cotton Mather (1663–1728)

around, because another neighbour, Alice Baylie, admitted that she had asked Joan whether she or her husband would die first. Joan had prudently refused to tell her on the grounds that her gift was already looked upon with suspicion.

Joan Wright was allowed to walk free, but her case shows how much the inhabitants of these small and tightly knit communities feared any kind of unusual abilities. It bears repeating that the horror of the Salem trials did not spring out of nowhere; Joan's case was just one of a series of trials across the colonies that set the stage for Salem. Both men and women were accused of witchcraft, and some of the accusations were little short of ludicrous. Eunice Cole of Massachusetts and New Hampshire was said to have turned a young boy into an ape and to have shapeshifted into a dog and an eagle; she was tried several times for various offences between 1647 and 1673 and finally imprisoned. John Godfrey of Massachusetts was another who suffered a bad reputation and was repeatedly brought to trial, once on the slender grounds that a witness thought he remembered seeing Godfrey yawning in church and revealing a witch's teat under his tongue. Godfrey was lucky; in 1659 he was acquitted of all charges, and in a later trial in 1666 he was acquitted on a technicality.

Not everyone was so fortunate. In 1685, Rebecca Fowler was brought to trial in Maryland, accused of causing illness and injury by witchcraft. She pleaded not guilty, but to no avail; she was hanged on 9th October. And the case of Goodwife Glover is especially poignant. Goodwife was an old Irish woman who spoke only Gaelic. Her daughter served as washerwoman to a family called Godwin, and when one of the six children accused her of stealing some linen, old Godwin

allegedly caused four of the children to start having fits. One of the ways of testing for a witch was to get him or her to recite the Lord's Prayer; failure to do so proved their allegiance to the Devil. Old Godwin failed the test because, as she later explained, she was a Roman Catholic and used to reciting the prayer in Latin, although even that was too hard for her in places. Also, as a Gaelic speaker, she simply did not know it in English.

The affair caught the attention of one of colonial America's principal intellectuals, Cotton Mather, who wrote a pamphlet about it. Despite Mather's predilection for science and rational thought, he had a strong superstitious streak that may be traced back to his Puritan beliefs; he was himself a minister. According to his report, the old lady did herself no favours by admitting that the poppets made of rags found in her house had a magical use. She put on a dramatic demonstration in court by wiping her spit on one of them, at which point one of the afflicted children promptly had more fits.

Old Godwin's case highlights the fatal misunderstandings that could arise from the mingling of cultures that was occurring among the colonists. Her testimony had to be given via a translator, and some of her terminology was ambiguous; for example, the Irish word for "spirit" and "good angel" were the same. But to Puritan thinking, a spirit was likely to be an imp from hell, especially in a case of witchcraft.

Old Godwin was condemned to be hanged. According to Mather, on her way to the gallows she warned that the children's sufferings would not end with her death because another woman was involved in them. Sure enough, the children went from bad to worse but, frustratingly, Mather does not bring his story to a conclusion. We are

LATE

Memorable Providences

Relating to

Witchcrafts and Poffeffions,

Clearly Manifefting,

Not only that there are Witches, but that Good Men (as well as others) may poffibly have their Lives fhortned by fuch evil Inftruments of Satan.

Written by *Cotton Mather* Minifter of the Gofpel at *Bofton* in *New-England*.

The Second Impreffion.

Recommended by the Reverend Mr. *Richar.* *Baxter* in *London*, and by the Minifters of *Bofton* and *Charleftown* in *New-England*.

LONDON,

Printed for *Tho. Parkhurft* at the *Bible* and *Three Crowns* in *Cheapfide* near *Mercers-* Chapel. 1691.

A pamphlet describing Late Memorable Providences Relating to Witchcrafts and Possessions.

The title page of Cotton Mather's The Wonders of the Invisible World.

The Wonders of the Invisible World.

OBSERVATIONS

As well *Historical* as *Theological*, upon the NATURE, the NUMBER, and the OPERATIONS of the

DEVILS.

Accompany'd with

I. Some Accounts of the Grievous Molestations, by DÆMONS and WITCHCRAFTS, which have lately annoy'd the Countrey; and the Trials of some eminent *Malefactors* Executed upon occasion thereof : with several Remarkable *Curiosities* therein occurring.

II. Some Counsils, Directing a due Improvement of the terrible things, lately done, by the Unusual & Amazing Range of EVIL SPIRITS, in Our Neighbourhood : & the methods to prevent the *Wrongs* which those *Evil Angels* may intend against all sorts of people among us; especially in Accusations of the Innocent.

III. Some Conjectures upon the great EVENTS, likely to befall, the WORLD in General, and NEW-ENGLAND in Particular; as also upon the Advances of the TIME, when we shall see BETTER DAYES.

IV. A short Narrative of a late Outrage committed by a knot of WITCHES in *Swedeland*, very much Resembling, and so far Explaining, *That* under which our parts of *America* have laboured !

V. THE DEVIL DISCOVERED : In a Brief Discourse upon those TEMPTATIONS, which are the more Ordinary *Devices* of the Wicked One.

By Cotton Mather.

Boston Printed, and Sold by *Benjamin Harris*, 1693.

As news of Tituba's tales of West Indian lore and practices got around, other young women joined the sessions. Elizabeth and Abigail were the youngest, the others ranging from 12 to 20 years old. All the attention they were receiving must have over-excited Elizabeth and Abigail, who began to show signs of hysteria…

left not knowing who the other woman was because Mather refused to name her; nor do we know whether the children ever recovered a normal state of health.

Satan in Salem

Cotton Mather also turns up in the Salem witch trials, one of the most dramatic and notorious affairs in the history of the witch hunts. All began innocently enough after a new minister, Samuel Parris, moved to Salem. His nine-year-old daughter Elizabeth and her cousin Abigail Williams, who was two years older, had the idea of conferring with Parris' West Indian slave Tituba to find out what their future husbands would do for a living. Tituba obliged, and appears to have gone on to regale the girls with stories from her home culture. As news of Tituba's tales of West Indian lore and practices got around, other young women joined the sessions. Elizabeth and Abigail were the youngest, the others ranging from 12 to 20 years old. All the attention they were receiving must have over-excited Elizabeth and Abigail, who began to show signs of hysteria, sobbing and convulsing.

Unable to account for such behaviour, adults simply looked on as the girls found that they could kick over the traces of their Puritan upbringing and get away with it. Elizabeth hurled a Bible across the room, and Abigail spoke rudely to a visiting minister in church. The older girls also started to affect strange behaviour. Only one man in Salem showed some common sense: John

Rev. Samuel
Parris was the
most notorious
villain in Salem
Witch Trials of
1692.

Tituba's tales alarm the children, who accuse her of being a witch.

Proctor looked with a jaundiced eye upon the girls' antics and recommended whipping them all until they behaved themselves. But for the godly Puritan ministers and doctor, there was only one explanation: the girls had been bewitched and were possessed by evil spirits.

Under close questioning, the girls began to name names, choosing the most vulnerable members of society, who were not in a position to fight back. They accused four women: Tituba; a beggar called Sarah Good; the elderly and crippled Sarah Osborne; and Martha Corey, who had an illegitimate mixed-race child. All but Tituba energetically denied the charges, but Tituba was beaten until she confessed to being a witch and, after being coached in what to say, provided some imaginative details about the local coven. She later retracted her confession, but received scant attention; the grim course of events was not affected.

Sarah Good was the first to be accused in court. Frustrated by her stubborn refusal to confess, Judge Hathorne had the girls called into court to identify her as one of their tormentors. At this point the girls invented a new trick, and pretended that they felt Sarah biting and pinching them. Since Sarah was demonstrably not doing anything of the kind, they claimed that she sent a spectre of herself to do the evil work. The girls used this technique on all subsequent victims, and soon all the accused women were in Boston jail, where old Sarah Osborne died.

The girls were dubbed "the afflicted" and, having been given verbal confirmation of their status as helpless victims, they continued to point the finger at various neighbours. However, a couple of them began to develop a bad conscience. Mary Warren was the maid to the Proctor family, who suffered particularly badly from the situation. Mr. and Mrs. Proctor were both accused of witchcraft and jailed, leaving Mary with their five children. An avaricious sheriff promptly took advantage and confiscated the Proctors' property, selling off some of their cattle and butchering others to sell as beef. Fifty-two neighbours signed a petition for the Proctors' release, but to no avail. Mary unburdened her doubts to her friends – who promptly turned around and named her a witch.

And so witch hysteria spread, with some adults joining "the afflicted" in accusing their neighbours. The primary fault of the witches was seen not as the maleficium they worked but the sin of signing a pact with the Devil. Cotton Mather weighed in to declare witchcraft "the most nefandous [abominable] high treason against the majesty on high." Then a new governor of the colony arrived. Sir William Phips set up a special court to deal with the growing backlog of witches before leaving to deal with what he saw as more important concerns.

Adults who came to their senses soon realized that they had best keep quiet. John Willard, a deputy constable of Salem, had arrested the first suspects but soon came to realize that they were innocent, and that the girls were the real evildoers. His protestations fell on deaf ears and, realizing his danger, he fled Salem. His escape was to no avail; he was soon picked up, accused, tried, and hanged on 19th August 1692.

As the girls' reputation as witch-hunters became known, the nightmare spread from Salem to the surrounding district. Here the girls faced a new problem: once they were outside their own locality, they did not know anybody's name. Rising to the challenge, they exercised their creativity and threw fresh fits, stating that the touch of a witch would cure them. In Andover,

Salem magistrates examine Rebecca Nurse, who pleaded innocent of using witchcraft to torment her young accusers. Rebecca was one of nineteen eventually executed.

things got so bad that the judge eventually refused to sign any more warrants and was himself accused of nine murders. He fled with his wife, but his brother was then indicted, his alleged crime being that he had incited a dog to practice maleficium. The dog was hanged.

One of the most shocking aspects of the Salem trials is that none of the girls other than Mary Warren and Sarah Churchill showed any compunction about the sufferings and deaths for which they were responsible. One of them is on record as saying that the girls "must have some sport." The financial aspect of the trials is also appalling. The accused had to pay for their time in jail, even if they were acquitted. Indeed, they were fleeced at every opportunity, there being a fee for a reprieve or discharge. The relatives of those who were hanged had to pay the hangman's fee. Many who were

Increase Mather (1639–1723)

poor or whose possessions had been seized were forced to remain in jail; some of them died there. And what of Tituba, whose innocent games with Elizabeth and Abigail had started the whole nightmare? She languished in jail until 1693, when someone whose name is lost to history bought her by paying the jail fees.

A final cruel irony is that, while those of the accused who protested their innocence were hanged, those who confessed were reprieved. Apparently it was deemed sufficient to admit to their crime against God, while the innocent were considered to be hardened in sin. About 185 people were accused, 19 hanged, and one 80-year-old man crushed to death over two days under a plank loaded with stones. By the end of 1692, a backlash had begun against "the afflicted." Increase Mather (Cotton Mather's father) criticized the evidence being accepted from the girls and, as others took up the cause, the mood changed. When Sir William

Phips' own wife was accused of witchcraft, he prohibited any further arrests of witches and released 49 of the 52 witches still imprisoned. Those who had been found guilty were reprieved.

The special court Phips had set up was dissolved.

Such a hideous series of events would not easily be forgotten. In January 1696, the Salem jurors issued a statement of apology, and a year

The memorial bench for Sarah Good, one victim of the Salem Witch Trials, in Salem, Massachusetts, United States.

later the colony joined in a day of fasting to demonstrate repentance. All the accused have now been officially pardoned, and in 2017 a memorial inscribed with the names of the executed was erected in Salem. The trials have also entered the Western imagination as the archetype of persecution of the innocent. In 1953, American playwright Arthur Miller unveiled *The Crucible,* a fictionalized account of the trials intended as an allegory of McCarthyism. The play has since become a classic of American theatre.

Although the horrors of the Salem trials and the dubious nature of the evidence caused shockwaves throughout the legal system, trials for witchcraft still took place. What changed was the perception of those in authority, as reflected in the Witchcraft Act of 1735. This piece of legislation redefined witchcraft as a fraudulent practice aimed at cheating the credulous. However, in the popular imagination the witch still had power to terrify, as the legend of the Bell Witch shows.

The story goes that the Bell Witch started plaguing farmer John Bell of Tennessee and his family in 1817. The entity involved acted like a poltergeist, but could also appear in human form or as a large black dog. Bell's wife, Lucy, treated the entity kindly and was not hurt, but the Bells' daughter Betsy was pinched and slapped. At one point the entity identified itself as the "witch" of Kate Batts, a neighbour with whom the Bells did not get on, and who disapproved of Betsy's engagement to another neighbour, Joshua Gardner. Things got so bad that Betsy called off her engagement in 1821, and the haunting stopped, but it started up again eight years later. This time the Bells did their best to ignore it, and eventually life returned to normal.

> The story goes that the Bell Witch started plaguing farmer John Bell of Tennessee and his family in 1817. The entity involved acted like a poltergeist, but could also appear in human form or as a large black dog.

The fullest account of the Bell Witch was published in 1894 by Martin V. Ingram, a newspaper editor. *An Authenticated History of the Famous Bell Witch* has been variously regarded as a work of historical fact, an imaginative fiction, or a folkloric study of popular beliefs of that earlier period. What it demonstrates without doubt is that, even as late as the end of the 19th century, there was still a ready audience in America for lurid tales of witches.

The End of the Witch Trials

In Europe, the trial and brutal execution of Urbain Grandier at Loudun in 1634 gave many intellectuals pause for thought. The nuns' evidence was as flimsy as that of the Salem girls, the pact document they produced being particularly ludicrous. By this time a fair few clergy and professional people had been caught up in witchcraft accusations across Europe, and in places the madness had engulfed entire communities. Scepticism began to replace credulity at about the same time as the new discipline of experimental science started to reshape the way the world was viewed. God and the Devil almost had to find new roles as the observation and understanding of natural forces grew among the elite educated classes.

In 1683, a commission in Calw, Germany, went so far as to speculate that the Devil himself had instigated the trials, so destructive had they been.

Even though people continued to be brought to trial for witchcraft, the accusations no longer included that of renouncing God and worshipping the Devil. Witch hunting was officially discouraged in Germany. In 1682, Louis XIV prohibited further witchcraft trials in France. They were officially ended in Austria in 1755, and in Hungary in 1768.

The last person to be executed as a witch in Europe was Anna Göldi in Switzerland. Anna had had a troubled life. She was made pregnant and abandoned by a mercenary, and her child died shortly after birth. She was accused of murder, pilloried and put under house arrest. However, Anna escaped and entered service with a rich family, the Zwickys. Here she began a relationship with the son and they had a child, although they were unable to marry because of their difference in status.

Anna moved on to employment with the Tschudi family, a move that brought about her downfall. When the Tschudis' young daughter found needles in her morning milk, Anna was instantly sacked. Two weeks later, another daughter vomited up more needles, and this time Anna was arrested. She was tortured until she confessed to having made a pact with the Devil, but renounced her statement once the torture stopped. That made no difference; she was sentenced to death by decapitation, which took place on 13th June 1782. During the trial, the idea of witchcraft was played down despite Anna's confession; the official charge was that of poisoning. Even at the time the trial was criticized as being a miscarriage of justice, not least because non-lethal poisoning did not incur the death penalty.

In England, the last person to be hanged as a witch was Alice Molland, who was executed in Heavitree, Devon in 1685. A scattering of further

Women accused of witchcraft were tortured with the aim of extracting a confession from them.

✝ *Exeter Castle Gate House, where the last four witches were tried and hung. Their names: Temperance Lloyd, Susanna Edwards, Mary Trembles and Alice Molland are given on this memorial plaque.*

indictments followed, the last being in 1717 in Leicestershire, when Jane Clerk was accused of witchcraft. The jury threw out the case. Finally, in 1735, a new statute replaced the Witchcraft Act of 1604. The law no longer punished witches since they were no longer believed in; instead, it criminalized anyone claiming to be a witch. The Act remained in force until 1951.

Lawless Revenge

Of course, a change in legislation was not likely to affect the beliefs of those who for three centuries had repeatedly been told to believe in satanic witchcraft. Unable as they now were to turn to the law, country folk resorted to their own rough justice. The results could be as lethal as those of the law, and there are several extremely unpleasant cases on record.

One of these tells the story of an impoverished old Hertfordshire woman, Ruth Osborne, and her husband, who had been reduced to living in a workhouse. When Ruth begged for some buttermilk from a dairy farmer, rather suitably called Butterfield, he refused. Ruth muttered that she would be revenged. Nothing happened until the following year, when Butterfield developed epilepsy and some of his calves fell ill. He left dairy farming and opened a pub, where some of his customers suggested that Ruth was a witch and had cursed him. They consulted a cunning woman, who confirmed their analysis, and thus began a campaign of harassment against

Finally, in 1735, a new statute replaced the Witchcraft Act of 1604. The law no longer punished witches since they were no longer believed in; instead, it criminalized anyone claiming to be a witch. The Act remained in force until 1951.

the Osbornes. Sensing trouble, the workhouse authorities hid the old couple in the local church, but Butterfield's mob routed them out, stripped them and flung them into a pond. The shock killed Ruth almost instantly, but her husband just managed to survive. In this case, an example was made of the instigators, and the ringleader was hanged in 1751.

The punishment seems not to have had the desired effect because, tragically, such brutal treatment of helpless victims was still happening a century later. In 1863, another man in his eighties was living in penury in Essex. He was known as Dummy because at some time in the past his tongue had been cut out; what's more, he was deaf. Somehow it was known that he was French, and the combination of disability and foreign origin was enough to make his neighbours view him with distrust. Despite that, Dummy worked as a cunning man, offering divination by dramatic hand gestures to questions jotted down on paper.

As is often the case, strong drink had a part to play in mob violence. When a local woman claimed that Dummy had cursed her with illness, she soon gathered a mob behind her who gave Dummy the same treatment that the Osbornes had suffered. Like poor Ruth Osborne, the frail old man died.

Even as late as the end of the 19th century, fears other than that of witchcraft could prove fatal. One dreadful sequence of events that occurred in County Tipperary, Ireland in 1895 was so horrendous that it was widely reported in both the Irish and British press.

Bridget Cleary was a woman of decided character who, after starting in humble circumstances, worked hard until she had set herself up as a dressmaker and milliner. She and her husband lived in a house that was said to have been built, rather unwisely, on a fairy rath or fort; such places were best avoided, as fairies did not take kindly to intruders. In 1895, Bridget fell ill with bronchitis and within a couple of weeks her condition had deteriorated so badly that the local priest administered the last rites. As it turned out, that was a good thing from the Catholic point of view.

Bridget's family seems to have taken her illness as a sign that the fairies had abducted the real woman, leaving a changeling in her place. Ignoring Bridget's fragile condition, they took what they must have seen as appropriate action. First, Bridget was made to drink a herbal milk drink while her cousins doused her in water, urine and hen's excrement. Then she was dragged to the fire and held over it to force the changeling to flee her body. That did not seem to work, so the following night her husband, Michael, took rather more drastic action, throwing lamp oil over her before setting her alight. He appears to have sincerely believed that the changeling would fly up the chimney.

Poor Bridget burned to death, and Michael kept vigil for three days and nights on the fairy fort, waiting in vain for his true wife to return to him. Eventually he buried the charred corpse, and questions began to be asked about his missing wife. Nine people were arrested; some were acquitted while others were sentenced. Although Michael still maintained that he had killed a changeling, and not Bridget, he served the longest sentence, spending 15 years in prison – plenty of time to reflect upon having murdered the woman he loved.

Despite these late tragedies, the world had changed profoundly since the first days of the witch hunts. The rise of science had led to

An elderly couple, Ruth Osborne and her husband, of Tring, Hertfordshire, are suspected of witchcraft and lynched by a mob: the ringleader, Colley, u chimneysweep, is executed.

industrialization, which had in turn caused towns and cities to expand dramatically. In the countryside, farming had become increasingly dependent on machines. Better lighting banished evocative twilight and the terrors of the night. As education became more readily available, reading began to replace the telling of tales, singing of songs and passing down of folklore. And, as the patterns of work and life altered, magic changed its forms of expression as well.

Exit the witch, enter the magician.

A search is conducted on the accused for a witch's mark at the Salem witch trials.

The Magician
in His Circle

Magic Changes Its Spots

AFTER THE WITCH TRIALS DIED AWAY, history records an apparent lull in magical activity until it burst forth anew in the late 19th century. Of course, cunning folk continued to work their charms, but apart from the kind of lawless lynchings mentioned previously, they did so without coming to the attention of the authorities. The change of law had allowed them to slip back into an obscurity that they had not enjoyed for three centuries.

As the rise of science brought a more materialistic outlook to the fore, and the industrial revolution replaced the old rhythms of life with new and brutal regulated working practices, magic itself began to shift ground. The ancient foundations of Christianity started to tremble under the assault of Darwin's theory of evolution, prompting many people to search for new kinds of spirituality. What's more, the intense focus of an industrial society on gaining material goods produced an inevitable reaction: a longing for a simpler, more natural life. The Romantic poets Wordsworth, Keats and Shelley eloquently expressed the heart's hunger for the grandeur of nature and the free expression of emotion. From this movement emerged a new view of the figure of the witch, one that was alluring and erotic. All these forces fed into what is generally termed the "occult revival" of the late 19th century.

But before delving into these seismic changes, which altered the entire magical landscape, it's necessary to dig back into the past. The occult revival was revolutionary in its way, but it drew on a magical tradition that can be traced back to the Graeco-Roman world.

> As the rise of science brought a more materialistic outlook to the fore, and the industrial revolution replaced the old rhythms of life with new and brutal regulated working practices, magic itself began to shift ground.

The Dancing Magician

In Chapter One, the Neoplatonists were introduced, culminating in Proclus and his brief treatise *On the Sacred Art,* in which he outlined a form of magic based on bringing together various natural substances and items all belonging to one particular planet in order to attract the particular powers and qualities of that god. For example, the magician wishing to attract love would appeal to the planet Venus with suitable prayers and rituals, using items made from her metal, copper; decorating the altar with her flowers (roses) and wearing green clothing and perhaps even including a caged dove or two.

Over the centuries, such works from the ancient world were forgotten and the actual manuscripts tended to vanish into monastery libraries – being places where learning was pursued. But then a chain of events led to many of these works being unearthed, dusted off and translated into Latin, the universal language of scholars.

Over time, Christianity had split into two forms, represented by Eastern and Western branches based in Constantinople and Rome, respectively. In 1438–39, Cosimo de' Medici of Florence hosted a grand Council intended to bring together the two branches in amity. That failed to occur, but something quite unexpected happened instead. Among the scholars attending from the Eastern Church was philosopher Gemistos Pletho, who studied and taught Neoplatonist thinking and advocated the worship of classical Greek gods rather than Christ. Pletho stayed on and continued teaching in Florence, attracting a group of scholars for whom his knowledge and access to ancient texts were revelatory. Cosimo, too, became

enthralled and began to send out agents to buy texts for his own library.

The drawback was that they were written in ancient Greek, a language unknown to European scholars. But in 1457, another luminary from Constantinople appeared in Florence. John Argyropoulos was also a philosopher, and was also willing to teach Greek. Cosimo sent to him a young man who he already knew had a talent for languages and a passion for philosophy: Marsilio Ficino (1433–99), a small, unassuming man who was destined to change history.

Ficino was the son of the doctor who treated Cosimo. As medicine at that time used astrology to determine the course of an illness and its treatment, Ficino imbibed astrological knowledge from an early age. His parents both had unusual powers, and he would relate the tale of his father receiving a dream vision that inspired him to cure a patient for no charge. Ficino's mother, Alessandra, had the gift of second sight. He thus inhabited a world in which magic was taken for granted.

When Cosimo came into possession of a rare manuscript containing virtually the complete works of Plato, he turned to Ficino to translate them. Ficino started work in 1463 and did not finish until about seven years later. The complete translation was published in 1484, with some of the Platonic Dialogues being supplemented by full-scale commentaries. This is perhaps Ficino's greatest achievement, and was certainly seen as such at the time. However, before Ficino could finish his massive work of translation, Cosimo received a manuscript of most of the *Corpus Hermeticum.* Believing this work to predate Plato, and aware that his own death was near, Cosimo ordered Ficino to break off and translate the

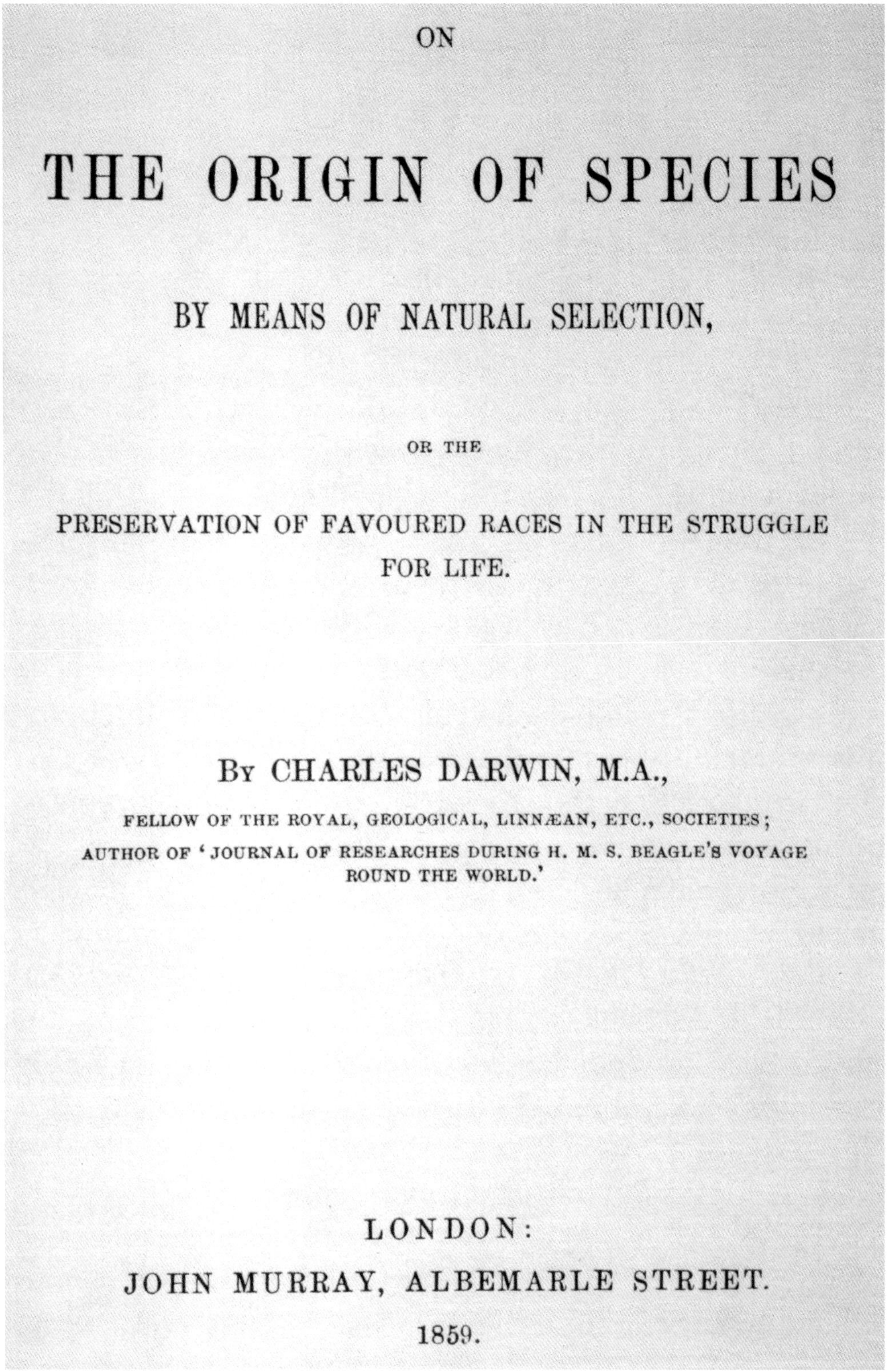

ON

THE ORIGIN OF SPECIES

BY MEANS OF NATURAL SELECTION,

OR THE

PRESERVATION OF FAVOURED RACES IN THE STRUGGLE
FOR LIFE.

By CHARLES DARWIN, M.A.,

FELLOW OF THE ROYAL, GEOLOGICAL, LINNÆAN, ETC., SOCIETIES;
AUTHOR OF 'JOURNAL OF RESEARCHES DURING H. M. S. BEAGLE'S VOYAGE
ROUND THE WORLD.'

LONDON:
JOHN MURRAY, ALBEMARLE STREET.
1859.

The title-page from Charles Darwin's revolutionary treatise on evolution, On The Origin Of Species By Means of Natural Selection.

Corpus instead. This Ficino did, going on to tackle many more obscure and esoteric texts, largely by Neoplatonists including Plotinus, Proclus and Iamblichus. Many of Ficino's translations were standard texts until the 19th century.

In 1488, Ficino translated Proclus' *On the Sacred Art,* discovering in the process how an ancient form of magic was worked. Proclus' aim was to unite his spirit with the ultimate God, known as the One. The work was called *theurgy,* and along the way the philosopher/magician came into contact with all kinds of beings in the spiritual world. From Iamblichus, Ficino learned that even the loftiest philosopher could with a clear conscience do magic for worldly ends, and he set to work with a will to practise magic on all levels.

Ficino had been ordained as a priest in 1473, and had to be careful what he said. He was too circumspect to set out clearly the implications of using Proclus' theurgic magic: that a full planetary ritual is the best way to absorb cosmic energy and bring oneself into harmony with the macrocosm. However, piecing together all the hints Ficino gives, it's easy enough to construct a ritual of which he surely would have approved. As well as all the elements mentioned above, it would include prayer, incantation and music. Ficino admits that language has power, especially when a prayer is uttered at the right moment and with strong emotion. Singing and music were also important parts of Ficino's magical regime.

Fortunately we have an account of a Ficinian planetary ritual as performed by a later admirer. Tommaso Campanella (1568–1639) was a monk who, among other grand ideas, dreamed of founding a city of the Sun run on astrological rules. He gained the ear of Pope Urban VIII, for whom he performed a variety of magical and astrological services, including a planetary ritual probably intended to alleviate the effects of an eclipse involving Mars and Saturn. Campanella draped a room in white silk and decorated it with branches, probably of laurel. Aromatic substances were sprinkled around. Two candles were lit to represent the Sun and Moon, and five torches for the planets. Participants wore planetary colours, and precious stones were offered. Music suitable to Jupiter and Venus was played, and astrologically distilled spirits were quaffed.

Ficino's position as a Christian priest who advocated Pagan philosophy, used magic and practised astrology caused some to doubt the orthodoxy of his beliefs. In 1489 he published – not without some anxiety – a compendium of advice on physical and spiritual health, the *Liber de Vita in Tres Libros* or *Three Books on Life.* This included instructions on making talismans, identifying one's daemon and using planetary influences. Despite Ficino's assurances that he advocated nothing that the Church would not approve, the Roman Curia looked unfavourably on the work. Ficino would have been in trouble, but influential friends came to his aid. His own bishop, Rainaldo Orsini, spoke up for him, and the great Venetian scholar and diplomat Ermolao Barbaro also seems to have swayed Pope Innocent VIII in Ficino's favour.

Although Ficino was circumspect about his magical activities, he was proud of his powers of exorcism and believed himself to have prophetic ability. He was accomplished on the lyre, and composed healing astrological songs for his friends. Ficino knew the Orphic Hymns, which were considered to be immensely potent for magic, and his friends dubbed him the Second Orpheus. He also revived (or invented) Orphic

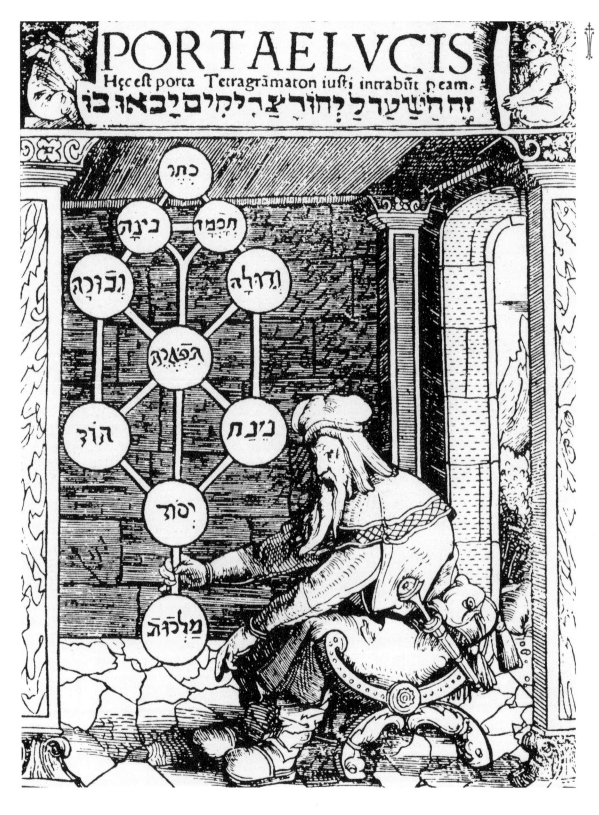

Kabbalah diagram of the Sefirothic Tree, showing the divine attributes in the Jewish mystical system enshrined in the Kabbalah. From Paulus Ricius' Portae Lucis, 1516. Each attribute is under the care of an angel.

dancing, a whirling movement intended to draw down benefic planetary influence. All Ficino's work – philosophical, religious, magical and astrological – had a single aim: to bring the soul close to God. Ficino's influence on the development of magic was enormous, passing into popular practice through Cornelius Agrippa (1486–1535), who based much of his writing on Ficino's work. However, Ficino's emphasis on spiritual aspiration did not prove attractive to many later magicians.

Ficino was not the only person in Florence working magic at that time. His friend Pico della Mirandola (1463–94), a well-educated nobleman, is important to the history of magic for two reasons. Intoxicated by the power of magic, in 1486 he penned his *Oration on the Dignity of Man*, in which he claimed unlimited powers for mankind. The only choice the magician had to make was whether to use his abilities for good or evil. In Pico's view, men could outdo the angels and achieve sublime spiritual heights. In effect, he created the blueprint for the learned magician who is afraid of nothing and subjugates both angels and demons to his will. Women, of course, were not even in the picture.

Pico learned Hebrew and introduced Kabbalistic ideas into European magic; it is thanks to him that such teachings have remained popular to this day. However, whether and how much Kabbalah (as it is commonly understood) reflects the original secret oral teachings is questionable.

Magic in Print

Ficino and Pico were working during the period when the invention of movable type made possible the mass production of printed books. This incredible innovation opened up all fields of learning to a vastly wider audience than laboriously hand-copied manuscripts could reach. Books of magic were among the first to be printed and circulated. They were known as *grimoires*, a word probably deriving from the old French word *grammaire*, meaning a book written in Latin. Such books covered all kinds of useful magical techniques, such as making talismans, casting spells, using magical ingredients and divining the future. But they also included the inherently dangerous topic of invoking supernatural beings and commanding their aid.

Grimoires had existed since the 5th or 4th centuries BCE, but now they came within the reach of the cunning folk who had previously claimed to learn their magic from the fairies. Some grimoires became extremely well known – even notorious. Such was the text known as Picatrix, a mediaeval Arabic work on astrology and the making of talismans. Popular even today is *The Key of Solomon*, a book of ritual magic describing lengthy purifications, sigils and the correct way to summon demons. *The Book of Abramelin the Sage* is also still in print in an English translation. This text describes an extremely ambitious ritual to summon the magician's guardian angel. Like all grimoires, the knowledge at which it hints will endow the magician with universal knowledge. He will be able to draw love to himself, find

A grimoire with hexagram. It was produced in southern Germany in the first half of 19th century.

Paracelsus (1493–1541) Swiss physician, botanist, alchemist, occultist, and astrologer. He believed in the Doctrine of Signatures, which held that the appearance of a plant indicated what illnesses it would cure. He also felt that the practice of alchemy should be directed towards the preparation of responsible, non-toxic medicines for curing disease and not as a means for manufacturing gold.

treasure and achieve positions of power while consorting with supernatural beings of all kinds. The latter two books were extremely influential on the teachings of the Golden Dawn, which we will be looking at later in this chapter.

As well as these texts, the origins of which are murky, some learned magicians who followed on from Ficino demonstrated their magical prowess by writing their own grimoires. Agrippa put a great deal of effort into both composing and revising his monumental *Three Books on Occult Philosophy* (1533) in which he covers a number of erudite subjects such as astrology, the four elements, the Kabbalah, mystical numerology and the names of God. Contemporary with Agrippa is Paracelsus (c.1493–1541), a German physician who was the first to prepare laudanum and pioneered

Paracelsus was the first to prepare laudanum and pioneered the use of chemicals in medicine. He was a man of his time and used astrology…

the use of chemicals in medicine. Paracelsus was a man of his time, and as such used astrology and invented a new alphabet for inscribing talismans. In *Philosophia Magna,* posthumously published in 1566, Paracelsus described elementals – entities existing in the four classical elements of earth, water, air and fire. He named them gnomes, undines, sylphs and salamanders, and they are still recognized in several magical systems today.

Royal Enchantments

Even though some of this elaborate, high or learned magic filtered through to the cunning folk via grimoires, it is clearly a world away from the simple charms and healing spells worked by those whose lives were not blessed with leisure and education. Learned magicians aimed high, believing that magical contact with angels and demons could teach them the secrets of the universe. Ficino had claimed that his magic was purely natural and had nothing to do with demons. All the same, he and Pico had set in motion a kind of magic that aggrandized its acolytes. Although learned, ceremonial magic was utterly unlike the kind of demonic witchcraft imagined during the witch trials, it exuded more than a whiff of peril because the magician consorted with dangerous spirits and claimed powers – such as knowledge of the future – that in the eyes of the Church rightfully belonged only to God. All of the learned magicians mentioned above faced severe trouble during their lives because their printed works laid them open to charges of heresy.

John Dee (1527–1608) was an English mathematician, astronomer, astrologer, occultist, navigator, and consultant to Queen Elizabeth I. He devoted much of his life to the study of alchemy, divination and Hermetic philosophy. One of the most learned men of his age, Dee was an ardent promoter of mathematics and a respected astronomer, as well as a leading expert in navigation. He devoted much time and effort in the last 30 years or so of his life to attempting to commune with angels in order to learn the universal language of creation and bring about the pre-apocalyptic unity of mankind.

That did not dissuade people in high places from consulting magicians. The polymath and magician John Dee (1527–1608) served two queens, Mary Tudor and her half-sister Elizabeth I. Although he is remembered primarily as a magician, Dee was hugely influential on several other disciplines. His deep interest in mathematics led to the introduction of Euclid into school curricula. He was learned in navigation and was the first to propose a national navy. Thanks to his knowledge of astronomy and astrology, he understood the need for calendar reform and he recommended the adoption of the Gregorian calendar almost two centuries before it was accepted in Britain. Dee suggested the creation of a Royal Library, an idea that finally came to pass as the British Library. His own collection of books numbered 4,000, whereas the library at the University of Cambridge at that time boasted only about 400.

Dee was almost too clever for his own good. He drew up the horoscope for Mary Tudor, but soon fell from favour far enough to be imprisoned for a while as a 'caller and conjuror of wicked and damned spirits'. When Elizabeth came to power, Dee came into favour once again. He drew up Elizabeth's personal horoscope and timed her coronation by astrology. The Queen occasionally came to visit Dee in his house at Mortlake, where he would expound the mysteries of his esoteric works such as *Monas Hieroglyphica,* an extremely abstruse text that defies simple explication.

But Dee never received the perks of royal patronage such as honours or high office. He was too deeply embroiled in the world of magic to be quite reputable. As time passed, Dee seems to have spent increasing amounts of time and energy attempting to contact angels. He was never able to do this himself, but relied on assistants, the most notorious of whom was Edward Kelley. This dubious person turned up at Mortlake one day, allegedly wearing a cap that concealed the fact that both his ears had been cropped – the sign of a forger. Kelley and Dee worked and travelled in Europe together for years, with Kelley offering royalty the secrets of alchemy. Possibly the two were spying for Elizabeth. What is certain is that they spent an unimaginable number of hours trying to contact spirits.

Kelley claimed that he first saw an angel, Uriel, in a crystal ball. Uriel instructed him on making wax seals engraved with mystical, protective sigils. The angel then dictated a series of magical squares, their spaces filling up slowly with numbers and letters from some unknown alphabet. This represented the angelic language, which came to be known as Enochian. In the 20th century, the notorious Aleister Crowley elaborated the language into a whole magical system.

Painstakingly piecing out messages from various angels who dictated letter by letter, Dee and Kelley worked from 1583 to 1587. The aim was for Dee to master the angelic language and thoroughly understand the hierarchical ranks of angels and their responsibilities; he would then be able to command them and achieve universal knowledge. Kelley could see the angels in Dee's obsidian "shew-stone," which is now on display in the British Museum, but despite careful preparation with prayer and purificatory practice, Dee never did. Eventually the elevated messages declined in tone, and a sordid suggestion of wife-swapping was made. Dee's wife not unnaturally objected, and it is unclear whether the angels were obeyed on that occasion. Whatever the case, Dee never mastered Enochian to the point of obtaining the knowledge he sought.

John Dee and Edward Kelley working magic together.

Elias Ashmole, Antiquary (Ashmolean Museum) and astrologer.

Dee and Kelley parted company in Prague in 1589. Dee returned home only to find that his library at Mortlake had been plundered. The tide of reputation had turned against him, and when the witch-fearing James I ascended the throne, Dee knew he had to keep a low profile. He ended his days living with his daughter Katherine, sometimes having to sell books to buy food. It is a shameful thought that one of Britain's truly great men should have had to endure such an ignominious old age – but at least he is still celebrated among magicians and esotericists.

The Invisible College

The strain of learned magic stemming from Ficino and Pico rippled outwards through various channels, and it is this kind of magic, rather than village cunning, that 19th-century occultists took for themselves and used as a basis for new movements and organizations. These in turn influenced 20th-century occultism, including the new vision of witchcraft introduced by Gerald Gardner, known as Wicca. The channels through which the ripples flowed are disparate, but we begin on familiar ground: with an astrologer advising royalty.

Elias Ashmole (1617–92) had a profound admiration for Dee. Ashmole, like Dee, was an educated man whose interests ranged widely, from antiquarianism to heraldry and history by way of astrology and alchemy. His remarkable diaries

Ashmole, like Dee, was an educated man whose interests ranged widely, from antiquarianism to heraldry and history by way of astrology and alchemy.

detail his astrological workings and make it clear that Ashmole rarely made a decision without consulting the heavens. He made a rather lucrative marriage in that fashion and, attending Parliament as an MP, noted the times of decisive moments in the House. Ashmole was also in demand for his amulets that dealt with vermin, and he reputedly had the secret of alchemy passed on to him.

Times had changed since Elizabeth's reign; James I had been succeeded by Charles I, who, as we have seen, found himself embroiled in a civil war with the Puritan Oliver Cromwell leading an army against him. The English Civil War was followed by the grim period of Cromwell's Protectorate, during which time any magical activities had to be practised very discreetly

Symbolic representation of the Rosy Cross, the symbol of the Rosicrucians.

indeed. But in 1660, Charles II ascended the throne and Ashmole, who had been living a retired life, became his astrological adviser. Charles was permanently short of money, and at one critical moment Ashmole gave the king a rather misleadingly positive forecast for his hopes of Parliament raising funds for him by increasing taxes.

During his lifetime, Ashmole was known as 'the English Merlin' and 'the greatest virtuoso that ever was known'. He was highly respected to the point of being loaded with honours for his work in various fields; in this, he was quite the opposite of Dee. Partly this seems to be because learned magic had become quite respectable. The King himself had an alchemical laboratory, yet in 1660 he founded the Royal Society for the scientific study of the natural world; Ashmole was a founder member. Far from being seen as illogical and in some sense unreal, magic was considered a valid form of enquiry into nature.

The Royal Society, although not itself a magical organization, is one symptom of a new movement to form societies that affected the magical world deeply, and still resonates today. One of the earliest references to Freemasonry occurs at this time, in Ashmole's diaries. His entry for 16th October 1646 reads: 'At 4H.30' I was made a Free Mason at Warrington in Lancashire, with Coll: Henry Manwaring of Karincham in Cheshire.' Freemasonry employs architectural symbolism and is an initiatory system, each initiate advancing through a succession of grades as far as he wishes. Freemasons are bound to keep silence about the Craft, which is a common feature of learned magic. The knowledge purveyed is deemed too powerful for the hoi polloi, and secrecy adds lustre to mystique. Both the grade system and the vow of secrecy influenced later occultism.

Secret societies even appear to have influenced the foundation of the Royal Society. Known as Invisible Colleges, they were mostly concerned not with magic or spiritual advancement but with an objective understanding of the world. However, as we have already seen, such knowledge could encompass alchemy and it is known that the Invisible College mentioned as early as 1645 by the natural philosopher Robert Boyle included at least two members who were interested in the subject.

Another source of influence on later magical organizations originated from a society so secret that it may not even have existed – the Invisible College of the Rose Cross Fraternity, more familiarly called the Rosicrucians. Known only through a couple of pamphlets published in 1614 and 1615, the Rosicrucian ideal was powerful enough to send many intellectuals throughout Europe in search of the invisible society. By the late 19th century, the Order of the Golden Dawn was claiming descent from the Rosicrucians, and eventually the invisible college came into full view in more than one form. To give just three examples: around 1865–67 Robert Wentworth Little founded the Societas Rosicruciana in Anglia, which required all its members also to be Freemasons. Quite different in aim and intention was the L'ordre de la Rose+Croix founded in 1892 by French novelist Joséphin Péladan (who became known as Sâr or High Priest Péladan). Peladan intended to revitalize the arts by infusing them with spirituality, and he organized six salons in Paris that attracted many creative people. He believed that artists were natural mystical initiates and that the arts could express all the mysteries of the Western esoteric traditions.

Across the Atlantic, in 1915, another mystic and novelist, Harvey Spencer Lewis, founded the Ancient Mystical Order Rosae Crucis (AMORC) in New York. The organization now has an international scope and a very large membership. Clearly the Rosicrucian ideal of reforming society along more spiritual lines still exerts a great attraction for many people, and similar societies continue to proliferate.

Goat-gods and Priests

The whiff of sulphur that was popularly thought to emanate from all magical practices increased the allure of the occult for those who were unsuited for the materialistic emphasis of 19th-century life. Alongside the organizations catering for the mystically inclined, a few individuals became well known, indeed notorious. Perhaps foremost amongst these was Alphonse Louis Constant, a Parisian shoemaker's son who adopted the pseudonym of Éliphas Lévi (1810–75).

Lévi was an eccentric character whose influence on modern esotericism cannot be overstated. Originally intending to become a Catholic priest, he entered a seminary and progressed through the system until, just as he was about to be ordained into the priesthood, he changed his mind and left. He had already reached deaconhood and continued to wear clerical robes. This was not the last time Lévi flirted with the Catholic life; he later

Lévi was an eccentric character whose influence on modern esotericism cannot be overstated. Originally intending to become a priest, he entered a seminary until he changed his mind.

spent some time in a monastery, but once again left. His love life was somewhat complicated, so his vows of chastity might have troubled his conscience.

Having tried religion, Lévi then threw himself into revolutionary political thinking, writing *The Bible of Liberty* in 1841; almost immediately, he was arrested and imprisoned. But politics provided no more satisfaction to his restless soul than Catholicism had, and in about 1850 he went through a midlife crisis that brought him on to his true path: esoteric studies. However, he never

A Knights Templar initiation scene, with an image showing Eliphas Lévi's Goat of Mendes on the altar.c.1860

The Sabbatic
Goat, *or* Goat
of Mendes,
*drawn by Eliphas
Lévi. Hand-
coloured print
from the 1896
edition of Levi's*
Transcendental
Magic.

quite lost his earlier enthusiasms, and worked them into the flood of occult books that began to pour from his pen. In his mind, magic became the key to spiritual and political freedom. Taking his inspiration from Pico's view of the magus attaining the secrets of the universe, Lévi dreamed of a circle of initiates who would wisely guide the affairs of humanity – an idea that proved immensely popular and that even today echoes through occultism.

Lévi wrote his most famous work, *Dogma and Ritual of High Magic* (two volumes, 1854 and 1856) after a visit to London during which he met English occultists. One of them, A.E. Waite – whom we shall meet again shortly – translated the book into English, and it is still in print. The book is an impressive work of synthesis, weaving together various strands of magical theory and practice drawn from the grimoires, Kabbalah and Tarot. Lévi worked

Eliphas Lévi, the French occultist and influential author, photographed on his deathbed.

out a system of correspondences between Tarot cards and the Kabbalistic Tree of Life that is still used. His mystical reading of the cards is largely responsible for their enduring popularity as a means of divination. Indeed, many aspects of magical ritual employed today stem from Lévi, such as his casting of a protective circle with invocations of helpful entities at the four points of the compass (east, south, west and north) and his use of magical instruments such as the sword and chalice. Lévi also influenced the theory of magic, emphasizing that willpower and intent are what produce effects, ritual merely serving to focus these inner powers.

So far, so good. Lévi took the Renaissance vision of the magus and updated it, adding a tinge of disreputability and radicalism, but maintaining the lofty spiritual aims. Unfortunately, he also chose to place as the frontispiece to the second volume of his masterwork an imaginative depiction of a supernatural being that combined features of the Greek god Pan, an Egyptian god of some kind, and Baphomet, the god whom the Knights Templars had been accused of worshipping. The resulting image is sometimes known as the Goat of Mendes, and it has enjoyed an afterlife that tends to skew the popular understanding of high magic.

Baphomet may originally have been nothing more than an inventive accusation to throw at the Templars, along with claims that they worshiped the deity in the form of a skull, a cat, or a head with three faces. The knights' descriptions, wrung out of them by torture, varied from confession to confession. Lévi's dramatic illustration shows a winged, androgynous goat-headed figure with cloven hooves, glaring eyes, a pentacle on its forehead and a flaming torch

between its large, curved horns. He meant it to symbolize the union of opposites, but he could hardly look more demonic. Hence it is not at all surprising that it has been widely misunderstood to represent the Devil, and that it has been closely linked with the Horned God that Wiccans

He meant it to symbolize the union of opposites, but he could hardly look more demonic. Hence it is not at all surprising that it has been widely misunderstood to represent the Devil, and that it has been closely linked with the Horned God that Wiccans worship.

worship. From there it is a small step to arrive back at the deluded viewpoint of the prosecutors during the witch trials: that witches and magicians worship and derive their power from the Devil – those of the present day just as much as their predecessors.

A Magical Day Dawns

Lévi as an individual was immensely influential on the development of high magic, inspiring such figures as Aleister Crowley. But the lonely magician in his circle was no longer the only image available to aspiring occultists. As urbanization developed during the 19th century, the possibility of like-minded people gathering together in organized societies increased. Those who were attracted to magic took the new movements towards spirituality and the romantic imagination and applied them to their practice. Thus it came about that in 1888 The Hermetic Order of the Golden Dawn was founded. A great deal of imagination went into its founding; the membership included several famous novelists and poets, and its rituals were designed to have a powerfully aesthetic impact. To the modern eye, the outfits worn by members are also unintentionally hilarious, mingling elements of ancient Egyptian costume with mediaeval fantasy.

The Golden Dawn was not the first esoteric order to come into existence during the 19th century, but it has been unquestionably the most influential. It has profoundly affected both

Samuel Liddell MacGregor Mathers, in Egyptian getup, performs a ritual in the Hermetic Order of the Golden Dawn.

high magic societies and witch covens in many ways, from the hierarchical way in which it was organized down to its members' fondness for dressing up.

The foundation story of the Golden Dawn is so unlikely that it is best taken with a hefty pinch of salt. Three of the founders – William Robert Woodman, William Wynn Westcott and Samuel Liddell Mathers – all held eminent positions in the Societas Rosicruciana, so they already came from a society claiming ancient descent. The fourth, a clergyman named Adolphus

Woodward, was the one who set the ball in motion. Woodward claimed that he had acquired of a set of 18th-century initiation rituals into a Masonic-like society. Along with them came some instructions in ritual magic that drew on Dee's writings, the Kabbalah, the Greek magical papyri and recent archaeological discoveries in Egypt. This heady brew of magic was written out in a 16th-century cipher.

Westcott and Mathers combined forces to decode the documents, then elaborated on the basic texts to produce a complete working description for the new order, including its hierarchy, teachings and rituals. As if all this wasn't exciting enough, Westcott announced that the manuscripts included the name and address of a German adept of a Rosicrucian order descended from the original fraternity – which, of course, almost certainly had never existed. Westcott claimed that he had written to the adept, a certain Anna Sprengel of Nuremberg, who had authorized him to found a new branch of the order.

On 1st March 1888, Westcott signed, on Frau Sprengel's behalf, a charter for the Hermetic Order of the Golden Dawn. Thus, at virtually a single stroke, the Golden Dawn was provided with an ancient lineage and a set of teachings that had allegedly been passed down for centuries. Woodford had died in 1887, and in 1891 Westcott announced the demise of Anna Sprengel and the severance from the German group. No further investigations into the veracity of his claims would therefore be worthwhile. Not to be outdone, in 1892 Mathers stated that during a visit to Paris he had been contacted by the Tibetan Brothers, who had formerly advised Madame Blavatsky, the colourful founder of the

Theosophical Society. Since Blavatsky had died in 1891, the mysterious Brothers had looked around and chosen Mathers as her successor, commanding him to found an inner order of the Golden Dawn with three further grades and to be known, perhaps inevitably, as the Rosy Cross.

The Golden Dawn admitted women on equal terms with men, thus opening the world of ritual magic to them virtually for the first time; admittedly, only small numbers could be accommodated, but the establishment of the principle was extremely important. Several remarkable women joined, including actress Florence Farr and theatre manager Annie Horniman, both of whose flair for drama may help account for the theatrical nature of the rituals and costuming that Golden Dawn members enjoyed. Horniman also established the Abbey Theatre in Dublin, which put on the plays of another Golden Dawn member, Irish poet W.B. Yeats.

The grade system was taken from Freemasonry and the teachings given to the outer order covered a broad range of esoteric subjects including astrology, Tarot and the Kabbalistic Tree of Life. This smorgasbord approach opened the way for later magical and witchcraft groups, which also mingle as many methods and deities as appeal to them. The inner order took the training to a higher level, focusing on techniques of operative magic that involved contacting spirits and deities. Group ceremonial was important at every level, and since the scripts for rituals still exist, some groups occasionally use them today. However, the Victorian language and verbosity are said to be somewhat turgid.

The teachings of the Golden Dawn were, of course, kept secret. However, as time passed, initiates began to think differently. Israel Regardie

joined an offshoot order, the Stella Matutina, but he began to disagree with the way it was led, so he left. In 1937 he broke his vow of secrecy and published the full teachings and rituals, thus bringing down on his head bitter recriminations. But the cat was out of the bag, and anyone could use as much of the Stella Matutina material as they wished.

One basic magical procedure elaborated by Mathers from Lévi's work is that of opening the magic circle by invoking guardian spirits at the four compass points, each time inscribing a pentagram on the air with the tip of a ceremonial dagger. The process is reversed at the end of proceedings. This ritual of summoning and banishing has been adapted in many forms, and is almost universally used by magicians and witches. The pentagram – which we first spotted on Lévi's Goat of Mendes figure – has now become the image most people recognize as denoting magic and witchcraft.

The use of consecrated tools originated with Freemasonry. Golden Dawn members were expected to make as much of their own working equipment and robes as they could; the National Library in Dublin has a fascinating and poignant display of some of Yeats' magical tools and notebooks. This aspect, too, of Golden Dawn teachings has been widely adopted, although nowadays witches and magicians are far more likely to buy their implements, since a market has proliferated to cater for practitioners' ever-increasing needs.

In a less positive way, the Golden Dawn serves to typify another characteristic of magical practitioners: they seldom agree for long, and are prone to breaking away to form separate groups that often continue to splinter.

> One basic magical procedure elaborated by Mathers from Lévi's work is that of opening the magic circle by invoking guardian spirits at the four compass points...

Considering that until the late 19th century both high magicians and cunning folk worked alone, the nature of what they do is perhaps best suited to solitude.

As Golden Dawn members developed their knowledge and practice, some doctrinal differences began to surface. Most members were Christian, but Mathers and his wife Moina turned to ancient Egyptian deities for inspiration. Combined with various clashes of personality, these disagreements were more than enough to split the order, which fissured repeatedly until, by 1909, four offshoots had been founded.

The Great Beast

One of these, the Argentum Astrum, was established by Aleister Crowley (1875–1947), probably the only 20th-century magician whose name is familiar to virtually everyone. Unfortunately, he delighted in cultivating an image that is entirely negative, thereby tainting the reputation of subsequent magical practitioners. Crowley reacted against a strict Christian upbringing by becoming a libertine, devoting himself to any and all pleasures including drug use and sex with both men and women.

Crowley's magical practice combined working with Dee's Enochian language and a variety of techniques from other sources, mingling them in true Golden Dawn style. In 1904 and 1907, Crowley wrote several books under the dictation of a disembodied voice that he claimed was an ancient Egyptian entity. The texts formed the basis of Crowley's magical system, which he called Thelema. Three principles underlie Thelema: the well-known aphorisms, "'Do what thou wilt' shall be the whole of the law," "Love is the law, love under will," and the charming "Every man and every woman is a star." Never one to underestimate his own importance, Crowley believed that he had been chosen as the prophet of a new age, the Age of Horus, during which humanity would use his principles to find its true destiny.

Unfortunately, Crowley failed to live up to such lofty ideals. He was amoral and narcissistic and, once he had run through his inheritance, a shameless sponger. He revelled in his bad image, adopting the nickname The Beast, which his mother had called him as a child, and making great play with the number 666, which, in Revelation 13:18, is said to be the number of the Beast. Most of his friendships and sexual partnerships ended badly, and some of Crowley's more vulnerable partners can only be described as victims. However, the magical system he invented is still in use. As with the Golden Dawn, the Argentum Astrum is structured as a series of grades, with the initiate working through various techniques such as Buddhist meditation, astral travel and contacting the guardian angel. The ultimate aim is to reach the grade of Ipsissimus, which represents a state of perfect harmony with the universal powers and therefore of absolute freedom.

Crowley died in poverty at Hastings in 1947; only about a dozen people attended his funeral in Brighton. However, his influence has proved to be vast. Gerald Gardner, the founder of Wicca, adapted some of Crowley's material to write his own witchcraft rituals. Several magical societies exist (as well as the Argentum Astrum) that base their teachings on Crowley's books. Crowley's louche image has appealed to a variety of figures in popular culture, including the filmmaker Kenneth Anger, and several novelists have based characters on him. In 1908, Somerset Maugham published *The Magician* after meeting Crowley and being unfavourably impressed. Crowley appeared in the novel as Oliver Haddo, the antihero upon whom Maugham gleefully wrought fictional vengeance. Crowley did not take kindly to this, and published a piece under the name Haddo in which he accused Maugham of plagiarism.

Crowley is difficult to assess, because his love of self-promotion means that even today he is seen as dangerously evil. The truth is less titillating and much more sordid. Although Crowley certainly did a great deal of harm to other people, it was not by magical means but by utter disregard for –

Aleister Crowley (1875–1947), writer, mountain-climber, drug-addict, artist and occultist, known to his own mother as "the Great Beast."

and in many cases, exploitation of – their feelings. What he did bequeath to future generations of witches and magicians was his need to be in the public eye. Even now there are those who seek the limelight by adopting grand titles, robing up and courting celebrity.

A New Vision of Witchcraft

One of the great cultural developments of the 19th century was that of educated people collecting folklore. The tales and customs that for centuries had brightened the hard lives of the working classes were now perceived as being in danger of dying out, thanks to the violent overturning of traditional ways of life caused by increasing industrialization and the growth of towns. The witch was of course a central and fascinating figure in folklore, but since the educated classes were no longer terrified believers in witchcraft, the image of the witch began to take on complexity.

On the one hand were those who embraced the new Age of Reason and condemned all previous beliefs as superstitious. The evil witch was also a useful fictional device, providing horror and drama to any plot. But even wicked witches began to regain the glamour that those of the Arthurian mythos had projected, as can clearly be seen in Victorian art, where forbidden desires could be safely expressed on canvas. Many of the images still circulating of Circe, Nimue and the like came from the Pre-Raphaelite Brotherhood, a group of

artists who came together in 1848 to revive the art and ideals of the mediaeval period. These lush and romantic images still emanate a perilous and alluring sensuality.

The male Pre-Raphaelite artist saw the witch as a femme fatale whose love could put a man's Christian soul in danger while giving him unimaginable pleasure. J.W. Waterhouse's *Circe* (1891) shows the witch-goddess enthroned, wearing a diaphanous gown and holding aloft a cup and wand; at her feet lies one of the pigs into which she had enchanted Odysseus' crew, while in the reflection of a mirror Odysseus himself looks extremely apprehensive. The image frequently accompanies articles and books about and by witches, as does Waterhouse's earlier canvas *The Magic Circle* (1886), which depicts a wild-haired witch in a desolate landscape, using her wand to cast a circle of fire around a steaming cauldron as several crows look on. Many a 21st-century witch would love to be as powerful, dangerous and beautiful as these women.

The witch was of course a central and fascinating figure in folklore…

J. W. Waterhouse's dramatic painting of Circe.

As time passed, the wicked witch slipped from adult fiction into the children's realm, degenerating into a mere figure of fright to terrify them into behaving well. However, the adults' witch was rehabilitated not only in art but also in a new vision of the past. In 1750, the Italian scholar and abbot Girolamo Tartarrotti published *Three Books on the Nocturnal Congress of the Lamia,* in which he put forth the novel theory that witchcraft represented the remains of Pagan beliefs and practices. He believed the nocturnal activities of those accused of witchcraft had nothing to do with satanic witchcraft; indeed, he did not believe in witchcraft as such. A collector of folklore, Jakob Grimm, took the theory a step further by arguing that Pagan traditions had been mixed up with images of the typical (imaginary) heretic, resulting in the image of the satanic witch.

In 1828, a German law professor, Karl Ernst Jarke, added his voice to the revisioning of the witch. Studying witch-trial records, he concluded that what the witches had been doing was practising as best they could what remained of an ancient Pagan religion. Jarke theorized that the religion had been labelled satanic during mediaeval times, and then gradually warped into actual devil-worship.

Finally, an actual historian entered the fray – again, a German. Franz Joseph Mone (1796–1871) refined the idea of an ancient religion by pinning it to the worship of Hecate and Dionysus, the classical Greek gods. Hecate is, as described in Chapter 1, a goddess of night and of witchcraft, while Dionysus was famously worshiped by female followers, the Maenads, who would enter an ecstatic trance state in which they ran wild on the mountainsides, reputedly suckling snakes and tearing fawns limb from limb. Mone theorized that

A Roman copy of a Greek relief showing the dance of Maenads (Florence, Italy).

this disreputable cult was disliked even in ancient times, and even more so once Christianity had prevailed; hence, its adherents were persecuted during the period of the witch trials. Despite being a historian, Mone – like his predecessors – declined to back up his arguments with firm evidence.

The God of the Witches

So far, despite shapeshifting into a worshiper of Pagan deities, the witch had retained her dangerous character. That was about to change, thanks to the efforts of another historian, a strong-minded Frenchman called Jules Michelet (1798–1874). He was an excellent historian who, unlike Jarke and Mone, made a thorough study of his source material – when it suited him. Michelet harboured a deep loathing for both the monarchy and the Roman Catholic church, and often interpreted his material to support arguments against them. From time to time, he would also scribble potboilers lacking any factual foundation to raise money for his serious projects.

While he was researching the period of the witch trials, Michelet became fascinated by the image of the witch and, taking in the idea of witches as Pagan worshippers, began to build an image of her as a free-spirited rebel (he always imagined witches as female). Michelet's witch was as antiestablishment as he was; she rebelled against any form of oppression and specifically that of women. Like the Romantic poets, she loved the natural world, and she was in all ways

thoroughly admirable and romantic. Michelet put his ideas into poetic prose in one of his hastily written potboilers, *La Sorcière*, published in 1862.

When it came to the question of whom the witch actually worshiped, Michelet got into a slight muddle. He reasoned that the witch's very nature meant that she adored a female goddess, a Great Goddess indeed, whom he originally identified as Isis. But then how to explain the worship of the Devil? Michelet claimed that the god the witches worshiped was a Pagan fertility deity, either Pan or Priapus. Since Pan has horns and cloven hooves, he more closely approximated the Christian Devil, whom Michelet decided the witches also venerated. However, Michelet's Satan was the ultimate rebel who had freed himself from the yoke of servitude to God, and who granted the ecstasy of freedom to his followers. Michelet's book was understandably ignored by academics, but it was a bestseller all the same, and can still be bought today.

One reader inspired by Michelet's book was an American campaigner for women's rights, Matilda Joslyn Gage. Like Michelet knocking out his potboilers, she wrote in a hurry and without undertaking research. In *Woman, Church and State* (1893), Gage embroidered the image of Michelet's witch as a rebel. Gage's witch is also a healer and a priestess of an ancient matriarchal religion, oppressed by Church and State alike.

Gage is also significant to the history of witchcraft because of her estimate of how many victims were burned as witches during the three centuries of the witch trials. Recklessly, she stated that 9 million women died – a figure that came from her imagination rather than from research, and which, because of her theory, ignored the men who went to the stake. Gage's millions are all too frequently quoted as fact even today in the Pagan community.

Initiation rites of the cult of Dionysus, fresco from the Villa Dei Mysteri, 1st century BCE.

Frontispiece to Michelet's
La Sorciere (1911 edition)
with a portrait of the
author and a depiction
of sensational goings-on,
matching his somewhat
extravagant text.

The *Piper at the Gates of Dawn from* The Wind in the Willows *(colour lithograph 1913) made by Paul Bramson.*

213

The idea of a prehistoric goddess-worshipping religion of peace and plenty had begun to take hold among scholars. A German classicist, Eduard Gerhard, had first put forward the idea in 1849, and by the late 19th century it had been taken up by the forceful and theatrical Cambridge academic Jane Ellen Harrison (1850–1928). This redoubtable woman has been described as the first female career academic, and she was also a pacifist and a feminist. These strong convictions informed her view that the original Greek religion was a matriarchal cult worshipping Hera, who was later reduced to a subservient role as the wife of Zeus, the ruler of the gods. Harrison's enduring contribution to the concept of matriarchal religion was to invent a triple goddess. In her view, worship of a great Earth goddess had involved seeing her in three aspects: Maiden, ruling the living world; Mother, queen of the underworld; and an unspecified third aspect.

In 1901, Sir Arthur Evans mooted his theory that his sensational excavations at Knossos in Crete revealed a society that worshiped a goddess; in effect, it looked as if he had found evidence of Harrison's ancient religion. Although both academic theories and archaeological evidence were debated and criticized among professional thinkers, their dramatic appeal meant that they lodged firmly in the popular mind, and they have remained there until the present day.

Meanwhile, poets and novelists gladly embraced the idea of a Great Goddess, identifying her either as Mother Nature or the Moon, ruled by the goddess Diana. The god Pan, too, became a staple of literature in the late 19th and early 20th centuries, reaching his apotheosis in the lyrical chapter "The Piper at the Gates of Dawn" in Kenneth Grahame's children's classic *The Wind in the Willows* (1908).

The Goddess of the Witches

All that was now required to complete a thrilling picture of Pagan witchcraft was for someone to discover that it was still being practised somewhere in Europe. This fell to an American of expansive and imaginative character, Charles Godfrey Leland (1824–1903). Leland was a journalist and a traveller. His outlook was romantic and he made a study of Traveller culture wherever he found it. He read widely in folklore, magic and witchcraft, and absorbed Michelet's romantic vision of a rebellious, goddess-worshipping witch.

In 1886, Leland settled in Florence, where he believed himself to have struck gold. He met a woman whom he knew only as Maddalena, who appears to have worked as a fortune-teller. She told him a rich variety of charms, invocations and tales of supernatural beings – the typical material of a cunning woman. Leland asked Maddalena to collect as much similar material as she could from her friends and acquaintances, which he wrote up in a couple of books. Along the way, Leland heard rumours of a witch Bible or gospel, the *Vangelo*, which he longed to possess. Maddalena, however, was evasive and when, after 11 years, she finally produced a manuscript, it was copied out in her own handwriting. She then vanished from Leland's life, leaving him to study and translate the work. He brought out the result in 1899, titling it *Aradia, Or, the Gospel of the Witches*.

That is the story as told by Leland. Whether *Aradia* is a genuine witch gospel, or something

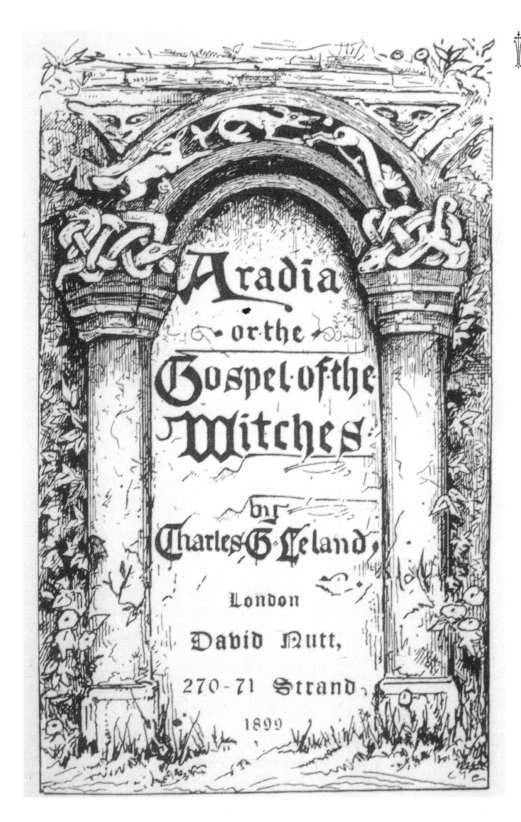

Title page of Leland's Aradia – *the gospel of the witches.*

Maddalena dreamed up knowing what Leland wanted, or whether Leland concocted it himself from genuine spells and his own imagination is up for debate. Maddalena does appear to have existed, but her disappearance at such a crucial moment is suspicious. What is certain is that the contents of *Aradia* rather suspiciously reflect Leland's own anti-authoritarian sentiments.

Aradia is a slim volume, and it made little impact when it was first published. However, it is hugely important to the history of witchcraft because of its influence on Wicca. Some of it was even absorbed word for word into the Wiccan liturgy, but its principle significance lies in the creation myth recounted in the first chapter. This peculiar piece of writing in both prose and verse mingles elements from the Bible with Leland's antiauthoritarian outlook. In the beginning, it is claimed that there was a goddess, Diana, sister of Lucifer, who had been banished from Heaven. They had a daughter, Aradia, whom Diana dispatched to Earth to succour the oppressed classes of the poor and needy, making rich people and churchmen suffer various disasters, including poisoning.

This myth is followed by instructions for holding a sabbat, which give a far more cheerful impression than the murderous orgies imagined during the witch trials. Crescent moon-shaped cakes are baked and consecrated, and a party follows, with feasting, dancing, singing and lovemaking – all done in the nude, in the balmy Italian night. Nudity appears to have been of vital significance to Leland, as it represented freedom from all oppressions:

> *And as the sign that ye are truly free,*
> *Ye shall be naked in your rites, both men*
> *And women also; this shall last until*
> *The last of your oppressors shall be dead…*

The rest of the book is a hotchpotch of spells and folklore. As a gospel of a religion, it is somewhat unimpressive, but the fact that it purports to prove the existence of a witch religion is of vital significance. Leland used the phrase, *"la vecchia religione"* – the old religion – either believing or wanting his readers to believe that he had discovered proof of the Pagan religion first mooted by Jarke. He was also "proving" the existence of Michelet's radical, rebellious witch and providing a creation myth to replace the confused ideas about just whom the witches worshiped.

Events were moving in the right direction for the development of an actual witch religion. The basic elements were in place: the goddess and god, the motivation, the romantic and pleasure-loving participants, the basic liturgy, and a good few spells covering basic needs such as attracting love or ensuring a good wine vintage. Far from being regarded either with fear and loathing, as during the witch trials, or considered a fraudulent nuisance to society, the witch had blossomed into a highly compelling and attractive character who kicked over the traces of propriety, celebrated life with whole-hearted glee, and punished her oppressors.

Meanwhile, the solitary learned magician casting protective circles and invoking demons and angels in his study had found friends and formed societies dedicated to a graded development of magical skills, dressing up for dramatic rituals and working on spiritual development in order to become one with the ultimate deity. Times had certainly changed.

Aleister Crowley in ritual dress.

Chapter Seven

The Once and Future Witch

God of the Year and Goddess of the Earth

AS THE 20TH CENTURY PROGRESSED through its early stages, the developments of the last 100 or so years were coalescing into a rich occult mix. Welsh and Irish myths and folklore were being given new life in English translations, while Irish poet W.B. Yeats contributed plays and poetry to a vibrant Celtic revival. Characters from Celtic folklore, such as Cerridwen the witch, were now reclaimed as Pagan deities. Madame Blavatsky had made Theosophy all the rage in both the US and Britain; indeed, her influence stretched as far as India. Sir James Frazer's monumental study of worldwide folklore, *The Golden Bough* (first published in 1890) caught the public imagination and reverberated through the arts for decades to come.

Frazer was an anthropologist who held the Victorian belief in progress. He applied this idea to the development of thought, seeking through his study of myth and folk customs to prove that human thinking advanced from belief in magic to faith in religion and onward to a triumphant appreciation of scientific rationality. Frazer took as his basic argument the theme of a dying god, claiming that all tales in which a god died and was resurrected in some form symbolized the annual withering and blooming of vegetation. He caused a scandal by including Christ in this thesis – a step too far that he was later forced to modify. According to Frazer, the myth of the dying god was once acted out in society in a regular ritual killing of a sacred king representing the god, whose blood would ensure the fertility of the land. He theorized that as time passed and human

> Rather than rejoicing smugly over their enlightened rational state, readers were strongly attracted to his lurid descriptions of fertility rituals focusing on sex and death.

sacrifice became unacceptable, substitutes were found until the ritual finally found expression in harmless folk practices.

Frazer's book did not have quite the effect that he had intended. Rather than rejoicing smugly over their enlightened rational state, readers were strongly attracted to his lurid descriptions of fertility rituals focusing on sex and death. Professional anthropologists were impressed at first, but later dismissed the work, since Frazer did not scruple to alter evidence to support his argument. But although *The Golden Bough* ought to be regarded largely as a work of the imagination, it inspired such powerful works as Joseph

Helena Petrovna Blavatsky (1831–1891), Russian mystic and writer.

The Theosophist *cover of the first number of Madame Blavatsky's house journal.*

Conrad's short novel *Heart of Darkness* (1899) and Igor Stravinsky's avant-garde ballet and orchestral work *The Rite of Spring* (1913). The book's theme of the dying god also found its way into Wicca and is still used in ritual.

The popularity of Frazer's work was part of the general blooming of interest in folklore that had begun earlier in the 19th century. The ancient Pagan world began to be seen as a refuge from the deracinated existence created by industrialized "progress". Seen through rose-coloured glasses, Paganism became a haven of traditional wisdom, a mystical connection to the land, and a lusty celebration of life. Festivals such as the Padstow 'Obby 'Oss Day were seen as surviving remnants of an ancient Pagan fertility religion, an interpretation that is still common despite the fact that most folk festivals cannot be traced back through more than a few centuries. The Padstow 'Obby 'Oss itself makes no appearance in local records or literary accounts of Cornish folklore until 1803, when the festival took a quite different form from today.

Strangely enough, it was an Egyptologist with a side interest in folklore who gave the English-speaking Pagan world its religion. Leland had claimed his *vecchia religione* only for Italy, but Margaret Murray (1862–1963) envisioned a European and British witch cult that worshiped a horned fertility god. Finding herself unable to excavate in Egypt during the First World War, Murray turned her formidable energy to investigating the folklore of her own country. She had read Frazer and been convinced by his vision of a cult surrounding the annual ritual sacrifice of a sacred king representing the natural world. When an acquaintance mentioned the theory that the victims of the witch trials had been practising

a Pagan religion, she put two and two together.

Unlike her most of her 19th-century forebears, Murray actually researched her subject. She read many of the sensational pamphlets published at the time of the trials and whatever other accounts of them existed in print, most of which had been published in the 19th century. Unfortunately, Murray failed to consider that the lurid confessions had been extracted under extreme duress; she took them as the literal truth. She also cherry-picked her evidence, omitting those aspects that did not fit in with her idea of the Pagan religion she was inventing.

Murray's method of constructing the rites of her witch cult remind one irresistibly of an archaeologist building a picture of a civilization from a random collection of potsherds. From Isobel Gowdie she took the term "coven" and applied it as standard to the groups of 13 witches (the number again gleaned from Gowdie) that she claimed once met all over the country. Such groups were subordinate to a Grand Master who exercised ultimate authority over a number of covens. Each one was led by a man known as the Devil, who would dress the part of incarnated horned god by wearing animal skins and a horned mask. The covens met to celebrate sabbats on the quarter days of Candlemas, May Day, Lammas and All-Hallows; in between times, business meetings known as *esbats* were conducted. During these gatherings, the coven worshiped their incarnate god, practised ritual sex, feasted, danced – and sacrificed young children and animals. All this fantasy was published in 1921 as *The Witch-Cult in Western Europe*.

Murray later modified her view somewhat, stating that the blood sacrifices were a result of Christian persecution of the cult. In a follow-up

Visitors and townsfolk take part each year in the festivities at the Padstow 'Obby 'Oss celebrations to herald in the month of May with ancient rites of spring.

book (*The God of the Witches*, 1931) aimed at the general reader rather than her academic peers, she emphasized the life-affirming aspects of the cult's rites. She also expanded her theory to include royalty in the cult membership. Murray claimed that kings such as William Rufus (c.1056-1100), who had been killed by an arrow while hunting in the New Forest, was a sacred king ritually and willingly sacrificed for the sake of the land's fertility. Other rather surprising candidates, such as Thomas à Becket and Joan of Arc, were also portrayed as substitute sacrifices for royalty.

Murray's apparent expertise in witchcraft history led to her being asked to contribute the entry on witchcraft for the *Encyclopaedia Britannica*. Her essay had a long life, and was published annually from 1929 to 1968. Murray's thesis was thus, unfortunately, given the status of reliable fact, reaching a wide audience. It had a profound impact on those who were reinventing witchcraft as a religion. Indeed, Murray's fantasy has entered the neoPagan imagination so deeply that it is hard to uproot. The fact that the academic world had, by the 1970s, made mincemeat of Murray's research methods and thesis has fallen on far too many deaf ears.

In 1939, another archaeologist appeared to unearth the final proof that the Pagan people of ancient times had worshiped an Earth Goddess. The find was made during an excavation of the Neolithic flint mines in Norfolk known as Grimes Graves. In charge was one A.L. Armstrong, who sensationally announced the discovery of a crudely carved chalk female figurine, placed upon an altar with a chalk bowl and phallus nearby. No more dramatic representation of an ancient fertility cult could be imagined, and the find was widely publicized.

Margaret Murray wrote an entry on witchcraft for the Encyclopaedia Britannica *that included some dubious information.*

Unfortunately, it is highly likely to have been faked. The archaeological community had its doubts right from the start, but no investigation was carried out until more than 50 years later, in 1991. Chalk cannot be dated, but several factors suggest that someone on Armstrong's team had carved the items either as a joke on him or with his connivance. The original find had not been recorded in his otherwise meticulous field notes, on a day when he had dismissed all his most experienced team members from the site.

Aerial view reconstruction drawing of Grimes Graves in circa 2000 BCE by Judith Dobie.

However, the long delay in checking the figurine's provenance allowed a whole generation to accept her as a fertility goddess of Earth, the ideal mate for Frazer and Murray's vegetation god.

> **According to Liddell, Pickingill was the Master of nine local covens, run along the lines laid out by Murray. No mere cunning man, Pickingill had an extensive knowledge of magical systems including Satanism and Islamic magic.**

Master of Nine Covens

As an example of how Murray's thesis entered into neoPagan mythology, we will look briefly at the life of a rural cunning man, George Pickingill (1816–1909). George lived in the Essex village of Canewdon, working as a farm labourer. Like most cunning folk, he practised his cunning alongside his regular occupation; but unlike the majority, he did not charge for his services – although some grateful clients paid him anyway. He practised the usual cunning skills of curing illnesses and finding lost or stolen property, and was well known for his ability to control animals. Locals also claimed that he would cadge beer out of farmers by threatening to lay a curse on their farm machinery.

All these details are known because the folklore scholar Eric Maple learned about Pickingill when he was researching folk beliefs and witchcraft in 19th-century Essex. He interviewed Canewdon residents who were old enough to remember Pickingill, and the stories about him had been passed down to younger generations.

So far, so unremarkable. However, in 1974, a writer named Bill Liddell brought out *The Pickingill Papers,* making rather extraordinary claims for the cunning man. According to Liddell, Pickingill was the Master of nine local covens, run along the lines laid out by Murray. No mere cunning man, Pickingill had an extensive knowledge of magical systems including Satanism and Islamic magic. He worked with Freemasons and Rosicrucians and, as an acknowledged authority on witchcraft and black magic, was consulted by occultists from as far afield as the US.

The Grimes Graves Goddess that was discovered in Norfolk. Originally thought to be Neolithic, there is speculation that it may have been forged.

Aleister Crowley himself had been initiated into one of Pickingill's covens.

Liddell claimed that Pickingill more or less single-handedly formed Wicca, the modern witchcraft religion. His covens practised ritual nudity, worshiped a Great Goddess, had three degrees of initiation and sported many other features that were central to Wicca. The salient point here is that Wicca was really the creation of one man, Gerald Gardner – but Liddell claimed that Gardner had merely inherited the religion. In the tradition established by Victorian scholars writing about witchcraft, Liddell scorned to offer any evidence for his wild claims. He never paused to consider that a steady succession of occult luminaries turning up in an Essex village to consult a farm labourer would have caused a national sensation. Nor did he see the absurdity of Pickingill, who by Maple's account had led a life of hard work and poverty, boasting a vast array of occult knowledge. Like Murray's books, *The Pickingill Papers* is still in print and considered authoritative by some contemporary Pagans.

The Poet's Triple Goddess

The complicated outline of the origins of Wicca should by now be clarifying, but there is one more major influence to discuss. As unlikely in his way as Pickingill the master occultist is Robert Graves, the celebrated poet and novelist. He wrote one of the most influential texts of the 20th century on

Wicca, and yet he claimed he was unmoved by "witchcraft, spiritualism, yoga, fortune-telling, automatic writing, and the like".

Graves was a firm believer in acting on inspiration. In 1944, he was working hard on a novel based on the Greek myth of Jason and the Argonauts when out of the blue a revelation struck him. Graves was jolted from the world of ancient Greece to the early history of Britain, and he began to write like a man possessed. Within three weeks he had completed a 70,000-word book, *The Roebuck in the Thicket*. He then set the manuscript aside for other work, returning to it a few years later and developing Frazer's idea of the sacrificial god-king into a rather morbid theory that every poet must accept his fate as a victim of the triple moon goddess. The book was published in 1948 as *The White Goddess*.

Graves subtitled the book "a historic grammar of poetic myth". In it, he demonstrates an eclectic knowledge of myth and literature that he interprets according to his own peculiar and eccentric character. Graves seems to have succumbed to the syndrome well known by every student who has immersed him or herself in a research topic: that of suddenly seeing it everywhere as an over-arching theory of everything.

As he began writing, Graves found himself drawn deeper and deeper into a labyrinth of complex revelations founded on the theory that true poetry is inspired by the triple moon goddess and that this goddess claims the absolute allegiance of real poets. He set out to prove that this had been so since prehistoric times, but that the matriarchal religion of the Goddess had been suppressed during the times of the Socratic Greek philosophers, so that knowledge of this ancient

Author Robert Graves photographed in the 1940s.

theme had been first distorted and then lost. The White Goddess envisioned by Graves is a complicated figure. He deeply admired and drew inspiration from Apuleius' classic invocation and description of Isis in *The Golden Ass,* in which she identifies herself as the beneficent, all-powerful queen of all the worlds. Graves writes of her as the triple moon goddess: "The New Moon is the white goddess of birth and growth; the Full Moon, the red goddess of love and battle; the Old Moon, the black goddess of death and divination." But the positive "white goddess of birth and growth" has a profoundly dark aspect. Her relationship with poets is truly terrifying.

No poet can hope to understand the nature of poetry unless he has had a vision of the Naked King crucified…and watched the dancers… with a monotonous chant of: "Kill! Kill! Kill!"…

The poet is in love with the White Goddess, with Truth…but she is also Blodeuwedd the Owl, lamp-eyed, hooting dismally, with her foul nest in the hollow of a tree, or Circe the pitiless falcon, or Lamia with her flickering tongue, or the snarling-chopped Sow goddess, or the mare-headed Rhiannon who feeds on raw flesh.

Graves was convinced that patriarchal religion was a spent force, and that the Goddess was ready to return. For that to happen, it was necessary for enough people to believe in her; she would draw sufficient strength and substance from that belief to manifest in the world. What Graves did not know was that the Goddess was already making her comeback.

When *The White Goddess* was first published in 1948, the literary establishment received it with a mixture of bafflement and enthusiastic appreciation. This was a time for unusual publications. Just about the time of the book's appearance, Gerald Gardner was working on his novel *High Magic's Aid,* which appeared in 1949. His flamboyant promotion of Wicca brought the existence of modern witchcraft to the public's attention, and by the early 1960s, the press was revelling in a salacious fascination with witches and the growing alternative society. Those developments coincided with the third edition of *The White Goddess* in 1961. This edition found more than one new audience: real Goddess worshippers, followed by the hippies.

The Father of the Witch

Where had these worshippers come from? The answer is from the religion of Wicca, which appears to have come about through a group of people getting together to perform mystical plays. However, Wicca entered the public consciousness thanks to the effort of one man.

Gerald Brosseau Gardner (1884–1964) has become known as the father of modern witchcraft. He was born into a well-to-do family and, after a childhood marred by asthma, enjoyed a respectable career, first as a manager of tea and rubber plantations in Asia, and then as a customs inspector in Malaya. In such exotic surroundings, Gardner developed a lively interest in Buddhism and local folklore, exhibiting such professionalism in his studies that his publications on the subjects were well regarded. He supplemented his interest in Eastern spirituality by studying Western organizations such as Freemasonry and the less exalted nudity movement known as naturism.

Gardner enjoyed a successful career, and was able to retire at the age of 52. He and his wife Donna moved first to London, and then in 1938 to the New Forest. In Christchurch, Gardner happened upon a Rosicrucian Theatre Company, which appeared to be right up his street. It was organized by a group known as the Crotona Fellowship, which gathered to study esoteric subjects. The members were, like Gardner, respectable and well-to-do people with a taste for the occult. Gardner joined the society and, once he got to know the members, he felt drawn to a particular group who seemed to have something else going on, about which they were very secretive. Prominent among them was a local celebrity and society hostess, Dorothy Clutterbuck. Her summer parties were glittering affairs graced by Conservative politicians and titled aristocrats; she was indeed a staunch Conservative. However, according to Gardner, she was also the High Priestess of a witch coven of the Old Religion such as Margaret Murray had described. This was what marked out the Crotona inner circle from their fellows.

Before long Gardner was initiated into the coven and began to take part in its rituals. With his scholarly instincts and history of publication, he longed to reveal the coven's existence to the outside world. However, the Witchcraft and Vagrancy Act of 1735 was still in force, making it illegal to announce that one was a witch. Gardner compromised by describing the coven's activities in disguised form in the novel mentioned above, *High Magic's Aid.* His coven was, understandably, a little uneasy about this, but Gardner wanted more publicity. He was well aware that there were no young people in the coven, and he worried that what the coven practised would die out.

In 1951, the Fraudulent Mediums Act replaced the old Witchcraft Act. This piece of legislation dropped the concept of witchcraft, instead making it illegal to falsely claim powers such as clairvoyance for financial gain. Thus, those who wished to describe themselves as witches could now safely do so. In 1954, Gardner triumphantly published *Witchcraft Today.* The book describes the rites of an old religion practised by witches for whom Gardner used the term "Wica." Within a decade the word had gained a second "c" to become Wicca, and was being used to describe the religion rather than its celebrants. Wicca is in fact the Old English term for a male witch, the female term being *wicce.* Why Gardner omitted one "c" is a mystery.

Gardner described his initiation as happening while he was still ignorant of what he was being initiated into:

> *I realized that I had stumbled upon something interesting; but I was half-initiated before the word, "Wica" which they used hit me like a thunderbolt, and I knew where I was, and that the Old Religion still existed. And so I found myself in the Circle, and there took the usual oath of secrecy, which bound me not to reveal certain things.*

Gardner compromised by describing the coven's activities in disguised form in the novel *High Magic's Aid.* His coven was, understandly, a little uneasy about this, but Gardner wanted more publicity. He was well aware that there were no young people in the coven…

Gardner wrote that the celebrants formed a coven that worked in the nude, worshipping a triple goddess and a god, celebrating the quarter days, and enjoying the pleasures of life, such as feasting. They used ritual tools and worked within a circle, more like ceremonial magicians than witches. Margaret Murray herself contributed an introduction to the book, even though the sabbats Gardner described lacked many of the distinguishing features of her imagined witch religion: the Devil himself, for one. The book was not regarded in academic circles as anything other than a fantasy, but it was a revelation to many of its lay readers.

What was the truth behind the unlikely story that Gardner told, of respectable and conservative citizens leading a secret life of lusty Pagan worship? Historian Philip Heselton has conducted thorough research into the origins of Gardner's group, and his conclusions show that Gardner considerably embroidered the facts. Why? Perhaps, fired by Murray's theory of a witch religion, Gardner in effect willed it into being. As it was, several of his group were not Pagan, but pious Christians. The woman who worked most closely with Gardner, whom he called "Dafo", was so alarmed by his reckless publicizing that she abandoned the group in 1952 in fear for her reputation.

Heselton has tentatively suggested that shared interests in such subjects as yoga and reincarnation drew the group together. Some are very likely to have read Leland and Murray and been so attracted to the idea of witchcraft that they began to believe they had been witches in previous lives. From there, a single step would take them to cobbling together some rituals and practices. Gardner was evidently a man of compelling personality, and before long he appears to have moulded the group of friends into a form that pleased him. And so a coven seems to have been born.

The Mother of Witchcraft

Despite the consternation caused in the New Forest group by Gardner's penchant for drawing attention to himself, his publications did attract some serious enquirers. Foremost amongst these was Doreen Valiente (1922–1999), who became known as the mother of modern witchcraft. Doreen had been aware since childhood that she possessed unusual powers. When her mother confided that a domineering colleague at work was bullying her, the 13-year-old Doreen asked her to obtain a lock of the woman's hair. Perhaps as a joke, her mother did so, and Doreen made a little doll stuffed with herbs; round this she wound the hair and then stuck in some black-headed pins. Soon afterwards, her mother's colleague complained of being harassed by a blackbird that appeared to be stalking her in her garden and pecked persistently on the window when she was indoors. Apparently unnerved by the blackbird's behaviour, the woman ceased her bullying behaviour.

Doreen seems to have picked up some magical knowledge by attending lectures and also from the public library, where she discovered Leland's *Aradia*. She was a natural mystic, for whom the worlds of twilight and moonlight revealed deep truths:

✠ *The Witches Cottage, a hut in Bricket Wood, England, was used by Gerald Gardner and his Bricket Wood Coven to perform rituals during the mid-20th century.*

…I went down to the bottom of the garden, one twilight…I looked at the surroundings in the twilight, and it was as if everything I could see became unreal and was the veil of something else.

I saw what people would call the world of everyday reality as unreal and saw behind it something that was real and very potent. I saw the force behind the world of form…Just for a moment I had experienced what was beyond

the physical. It was beautiful, wonderful. It wasn't frightening. That, I think, shaped my world a lot.

Once reports of witchcraft began to seep into the press from 1951 onwards, Valiente began collecting cuttings, which she kept in scrapbooks. She was already involved in magical practices derived from the Golden Dawn, having come into possession of a series of notebooks made

Wicker statue of a horned man with pan pipes outside Museum of Witchcraft and Magic in Boscastle, Cornwall, UK.

by an initiate, together with some ritual tools. Although she was never initiated into the order, she appears to have worked some rituals with a friend. Valiente also read voraciously, ordering books from her local library and occasionally coming across rare and unusual items such as Aleister Crowley's *Magick in Theory and Practice.* She had a highly developed critical ability, and was not fooled by the misinformation and empty words that plagued – and still plague – the world of magical practitioners.

In the autumn of 1952, Valiente read an article called "Witchcraft in Britain" in *Illustrated,* a popular magazine. Included was a claim that a New Forest coven had performed a ritual during the war to repel a threatened invasion. Fascinated, Valiente wrote to a man called Cecil Williamson, who had been mentioned in the article, and he passed on her letter to Gardner. Williamson and Gardner had worked together, Williamson having

Included was a claim that a New Forest coven had performed a ritual during the war to repel a threatened invasion.

founded a museum of Magic and Witchcraft on the Isle of Man, at which Gardner acted as resident witch. The history of the museum is complex, involving several moves, but it still exists in Boscastle, Cornwall.

The Book of Shadows

By 1953, Gardner had initiated Valiente into the coven and, as time passed, he made her his High Priestess. Valiente was by this time extremely well read in magic, and during her initiation she recognized phrasing from both Aleister Crowley's *The Book of the Law* and Leland's *Aradia.* Gardner was not at all pleased when she challenged him on this. His coven worked from what he called *The Book of Shadows,* which he claimed to be an original document. According to Gardner, all traditional witches had kept a *Book of Shadows,* a personal record of magical workings compiled throughout their lives. Gardner's *Book* described a cycle of rituals for the coven to follow. It included detailed instructions for initiations into three grades of witchcraft, the celebration of the various festivals throughout the year, and the correct use of ritual tools such as the athame (a blunt knife), the sword and the cords. Each witch was expected to make his or her own copy of the *Book of Shadows* – a laborious business, as it meant copying Gardner's text by hand.

Annoyed though Gardner might be at Valiente's perceptiveness, he recognized talent when he saw it and encouraged Valiente to improve the *Book.* Indeed, it is questionable that he would have been able to stop her, for Valiente was at least as headstrong a personality as Gardner. She is responsible for much of the finest writing in the *Book of Shadows*, and she also made some firm editorial decisions about its content, excising much of the Crowley material.

The contents of the *Book* reveal that, as stated above, Gardner and Valiente drew upon Leland's material, including – as we have seen – his emphasis on witches celebrating their sabbats in the nude. Valiente also left in some of Leland's phrases when she rewrote Gardner's *Charge of the Goddess*, producing a beautiful piece that inspires Wiccans even today. The *Charge* blends instructions for worship with lyrical promises of divine favour and the injunction – surely unique among religions – to enjoy the pleasures of the flesh and appetite. In later years, Valiente was amused to find that many witches regarded her work as an ancient piece of lore handed down orally across generations of secret Goddess worshippers.

The *Book* went through several versions as Gardner's coven developed their material and was mostly kept secret, although Gardner did publish some extracts. Such a document was, of course, invaluable to interested parties wishing to set up their own covens, and pirated versions leaked out. Finally, Janet and Stuart Farrar, a couple of Gardnerian witches who ran their own coven, made the decision to publish the whole book. Doreen Valiente assisted them and, in 1981, they published *Eight Sabbats for Witches*, in which they expanded upon the original material, elucidating it and incorporating their own outlook. Gardner had died in 1964, and his New Forest coven was a thing of the past. All the same, the emergence of the *Book of Shadows* into the public eye proved quite controversial among the Pagan community.

Valiente without Gardner

The publication of *Witchcraft Today* had offered Gardner an opportunity to enjoy publicity, which he pursued with an enthusiasm that his witch friends found alarming, even dangerous. Gardner was eccentric and striking in appearance; tall and tanned, he grew a goatee beard and a shock of white hair, and his blue eyes were bright in his craggy face; he sported several tattoos and liked a touch of dramatic jewellery. His enthusiasm for nudity in naturist camps and covens was misinterpreted, this being a period when the popular press found it impossible not to imagine that a gathering of naked people implied a mass orgy. All in all, Gardner was a gift to journalists and documentary makers, who began to take a somewhat prurient interest in the subject of naked witches meeting by night for mystic rituals that surely, in their eyes, involved non-marital sex. After all, sex sells newspapers.

By 1957, Gardner's coven had hit on a way to rein him in. They drew up a set of rules to protect the secrecy of their practices and insisted on consultation before any drastic steps were taken. Gardner attempted an outflanking manoeuvre, producing with a flourish a set of "traditional", pre-existing laws that, among other injunctions, restricted the High Priestess's powers. This flimsy deception did not fool Valiente, who, along with several others, simply left the coven.

It is hardly surprising that press attention caused a rift in Gardner's coven. Magical societies are prone to schism, as vividly illustrated by the

Golden Dawn. Perhaps that is because they attract unusual personalities with powerful convictions who do not necessarily get on well together. But Gardner had performed a great service to Wicca, no matter what one might think of the way he did so. He had brought witchcraft into the light – a new witchcraft stripped of all satanic overtones, celebrating a connection to the agricultural year and suggestive of a simple life deeply attractive to those disillusioned by the horrors of World War II and searching for a new spiritual meaning to life.

Gardner continued to court publicity, with the result that increasing numbers of people sought him out for initiation. Gardner trained the most suitable initiates to start their own covens, and so the witch religion he had founded spread like wildfire across Britain.

Once she had freed herself from what she and other coven members perceived as Gardner's overbearing manner, Valiente worked with a number of other witches. She also continued to read avidly, and conducted profoundly useful research into the recent history of witchcraft. Valiente was a well-grounded and energetic woman who, unlike many witches who courted the limelight during this period, never claimed an impressive ancestry for her practice. She had a talent for writing, which she expressed in poetry, short stories and a series of books that are among the most useful and informative publications on witchcraft.

Valiente was an early advocate for the idea that the initiatory system into a coven was not the only path to witchcraft. In *Witchcraft for Tomorrow* (1978), she included a *Book of Shadows* for solitary witches, including a ritual of self-initiation. This opened up the practice of witchcraft to those who for various reasons were unable to join a coven.

Valiente was well aware that the diffuse nature of the witch community was a weakness, and she worked towards strengthening it by the creation of centralized organizations offering publications, support and informed research. To this end, she was active in forming the Witchcraft Research Association in 1964, which published its own newsletter, *Pentagram*. The Association did not last long, but it had cleared the way for other, more successful, organizations such as the Centre for Pagan Studies, founded in 1995, with which Valiente involved herself toward the end of her life. The Doreen Valiente Foundation was created after her death in 1999 to take responsibility for the considerable collection of magical artefacts that she had bequeathed to her friend and final High Priest, John Belham-Payne.

Valiente's contributions to the development of modern witchcraft are immensely important. She played a crucial part in making Gardner's Wicca a success, and her liturgical writings are widely used and much loved. Her biographer, Philip Heselton, comments that her importance lies in the way "she turned what had been a rather poorly interpreted set of practices and beliefs under Gerald Gardner into a mature and intellectually rigorous religion, which she placed firmly in the land from which it grew." Her publications remain among the most accessible and practical in the field, although, as with all books on witchcraft (including this one), the reader should exercise his or her judgement. Valiente is the first witch to be honoured with a blue plaque, unveiled on her Brighton flat at midsummer 2013. Thanks to the Doreen Valiente Foundation, her work continues.

The Witch of the White Goddess

One of the people with whom Valiente worked was a witch who adopted the name Robert Cochrane (1931–1966). Ever since Gardner had claimed that he had discovered a traditional coven in the New Forest, the way had been open for others to come forward and say that they had inherited ancient knowledge from different covens. Cochrane was one of these. Born Roy Bowers, he asserted that his family had practised witchcraft for centuries, and that he had been initiated either by an aunt or a male relative (his story varied). He told rather sensational tales of ancestors having been hanged for witchcraft, and of his grandparents converting to Methodism only to be cursed for doing so by his great-grandfather, the last Grand Master of a Staffordshire group of covens. When considering these claims, it should be kept in mind that Cochrane became known for his habit of deliberately misleading people. He believed that this would make it impossible for anyone to manipulate him, and called his technique "grey magic".

What is clear is that Cochrane had read and deeply absorbed *The White Goddess;* toward the end of his short life he even corresponded with Graves. In 1962, he and two friends placed an advertisement in the Manchester *Guardian* asking for anyone interested in the ideas of *The White Goddess* to contact them. Thus he formed a coven (his second – his first had broken up after disagreements), which he called the Clan of Tubal Cain. Cochrane had once worked as a blacksmith,

hence the adoption of the Biblical smith's name.

Doreen Valiente met Cochrane and his wife, Jane, in 1964, after some friends had suggested they get together. She was impressed with the young man, who was handsome, intelligent and possessed of great charisma. Cochrane explained that the witchcraft his Clan practised was very different from Gardner's. The coven wore robes and preferred to work outdoors. Cochrane believed his witchcraft to be an extension of the ancient Mystery religions, such as that of Eleusis. However, like Wiccans, his Clan kept the seasonal sabbats, cast a circle with the four elemental quarters marked, and worshiped a horned god and a goddess. In other words, Cochrane's witchcraft appeared to derive quite a few elements from Wicca. Cochrane had also deeply imbibed Graves' idea of the triple goddess and the yearly ritual death of the sacred king, and his clan was organized as described by Margaret Murray, with a Devil and a Maid. The feel of Cochrane's witchcraft, though, was unique to him.

Valiente gave one of the few eyewitness accounts of the Clan's rituals, which she described as "shamanistic". They were physically demanding, but participants often reached a euphoric state. One in particular embedded itself in Valiente's memory, a Halloween celebration held high on the Sussex downs. After the circle had been drawn, the participants danced and chanted, circling faster and faster as excitement rose. Valiente saw a green, fiery light spreading across the circle until the witches collapsed in exhaustion.

Although Valiente suspected that Cochrane was making up such rituals on the spur of the moment rather than following the ancient tradition he claimed, she valued them for their effectiveness. But sadly, Cochrane began to alienate his coven in a number of ways. He would invite strangers to join the rituals, which most coven members found disturbing, and he became increasingly autocratic. Cochrane loathed Gardner and his followers, and delighted in producing articles attacking them. Valiente, who believed that there was room in the witch community for many ways of working, finally left Cochrane's coven because of his attitude. By this time, Cochrane had already started an affair with a coven member, to which his wife reacted by divorcing him. The coven broke up and he was left on his own.

Cochrane's version of witchcraft was much darker than Wicca, following as he did a vision of Graves' White Goddess as a lethal deity demanding suffering and sacrifice from her followers. He was also making occasional use of hellebore and belladonna as hallucinogens, a practice that was extremely perilous because even a small amount of either plant can be deadly. Abandoned by his wife and coven, Cochrane struggled on alone for a while, but in 1966 he took his own life.

Much romance has grown up around Cochrane's death, with many believing that he saw himself as a willing sacrifice to the White Goddess. What is sure is that he killed himself at the ritually appropriate moment of the Summer Solstice, and that he prepared his death carefully. During May and June he had obtained Librium from his doctor three times and stockpiled it, for reducing convulsions caused by the lethal dose of belladonna and hellebore he took. He wrote of his intention to commit suicide while of sound mind, and even left a note for the coroner stating unambiguously, "This is a carefully prepared suicide..."

Cochrane's death was a huge loss to the developing witchcraft scene. Intelligent and

Sadly, Cochrane began to alienate his coven in a number of ways. He would invite strangers to join the rituals, which most coven members found disturbing, and he became increasingly autocratic. Cochrane loathed Gardner and his followers, and delighted in producing articles attacking them.

creative, he brought fresh ideas and effective working practices that introduced greater spontaneity into the carefully staged rituals in which Wicca specialized. As it is, he left letters and short articles, and a witchcraft tradition developed from the way he worked that is still thriving – although its practitioners tend to keep a lower profile than many other contemporary witches.

Witches in the Limelight

Gerald Gardner was far from the last witch to have had his fingers burned by his avid pursuit of publicity. Hot on his heels came a charismatic young man called Alex Sanders. He caused a minor sensation in 1962 by inviting reporters from his local paper, the *Manchester Evening Chronicle and News*, to witness a witchcraft ritual on Alderley Edge in Cheshire. In fact, at this point Sanders seems to have known little about witchcraft, since he based his ritual on Egyptian material.

Naturally enough, the story that was published used terms such as "black magic", which did not go down well in the growing Wiccan community. Due to the rather lurid newspaper report, Sanders lost his job, but he did not give up. Somehow he got hold of a version of Gardner's *Book of Shadows*, which he altered to his own satisfaction before claiming that it had been handed down to him as the successor of (yet another) old tradition of witchcraft. In 1967, Sanders married a girl 20 years his junior in a well-publicized Wiccan ceremony. Maxine Sanders was an ethereal-looking beauty

with long blonde hair and, as such, ideal press fodder. Nor was she averse to being photographed while working with her coven in the nude.

The Sanders couple moved to London, where they adopted the grandiose titles King and Queen of the Witches. They became the preferred people for the press to approach for information on esoteric matters, and they trained a series of witches to found other covens. Sanders came up with the term "Alexandrian" to describe the tradition he had founded. He included aspects of high magic from the Golden Dawn teachings and the Kabbalah, and he also used Tarot cards. This expansion of material, along with the Sanders' vigorous founding of covens across the country, has proved to be their legacy to what has become known as the Craft.

The Sanders separated in 1973, with Maxine continuing to run a coven and teach while Alex retired to Sussex. He appears to have spent much time reflecting on his life; in a magazine article in 1979 he expressed regret for any harm he might have caused. Sanders continued to work with magical orders in a quiet way until his death from lung cancer in 1988.

Witches over America

Alexandrian witchcraft would hardly have achieved the success it did had it not ridden on the coattails of the 1960s counterculture centred in "swinging" London. Hippies were already dressing up in exotic clothes and delving into

Eastern religions and drugs, and witchcraft blended effortlessly into the scene. The same was true in the United States. Wicca was introduced to New York in 1962 by Raymond and Rosemary Buckland, and as it took hold, its adherents began to mix countercultural ideas and influences with it.

One of the most influential of these ideas was that of feminism, which was taken up by a Hungarian immigrant, Zsuzsanna Budapest. Enthused by the idea of a specifically feminine spirituality, Budapest conceived the idea of Dianic witchcraft, which was open only to women. Dianic witches also held strong political convictions, standing against patriarchy and militarism and for environmental protection. It hardly needs to be said that traditional Gardnerians abhorred the idea that men should be excluded, holding as they did that the energies of both male and female were fundamental to the raising of witch power.

Happily, a solution was arrived at by Miriam Simos, who had been trained by Gardnerians but was also in accord with Budapest's radicalized feminism. Simos adopted the poetic name of Starhawk, and in one of the most influential witchcraft books of the 20th-century, *Spiral Dance* (1979), she described covens as creative places in which both women and men could practise self-development techniques that would help develop their magical skills. Several of the exercises she suggests might have come straight from popular psychology books of that period. These American ideas passed rapidly back across the Atlantic, transforming Gardner's original Craft almost beyond recognition. The New Age movement made it acceptable to experiment with any and all techniques available, and the Craft as it now exists is one of bewildering variety. It is also quite big

business, with Pagan shops selling both mass-produced and individually crafted materials and tools. While many uninformed people still think of witchcraft as devil-worship or – at best – an ancient Pagan religion à la Murray, the Craft is increasingly mainstream.

Evolving Magic

Both witchcraft and ceremonial magic continue to change and evolve at what appears to be an ever-increasing pace, so almost anything written about "recent developments" quickly goes out of date. Now that both witchcraft and magic have been reinvented and can be discussed openly, they seem to be attracting more enthusiasts than ever. While it is all but impossible to estimate the numbers of those practicing witchcraft, every media story results in new adherents. Social media have enabled communications to burgeon; groups organize events, and those who work alone through circumstance or choice can still feel involved in a virtual community. At the time of writing, there was a move away from organized covens and orders, with their reliance on hierarchy and set ritual. The web has made possible online instruction in a plethora of techniques without any geographical limitations, and opened up a vast range of information of varying quality. There is also a worldwide market of magical merchandise.

In the real world, environmental concerns have taken their place in Wiccan and magical thinking, with some choosing to use magical techniques in support of activist causes. The pendulum is swinging away from the virtual world of the web, with increasing numbers of practitioners revaluing the direct experience of witchcraft and magic. Some are reaching back in time to the way the cunning folk worked, stripping away ceremony to find magic in their immediate surroundings, whether in the city or the country. Doreen Valiente wrote, "Magic, indeed, is all around us, in stones, flowers, stars, the dawn wind and the sunset cloud; all we need is the ability to see and understand." Many Wiccans and magicians are finding that developing a sense of communion with the surrounding world is deeply sustaining. Direct experience is found to be infinitely more satisfying than staring at a screen. The emphasis is on what magic feels like, which can range from meditative quiet to bliss or an awed sense of numinosity. After all, Wiccans and magicians practise because magic and witchcraft are life-enhancing. Gerald Gardner affirmed of Wicca that "...the spirit of wonder dwells in it."

The witch is no longer a fear-inspiring hag. Instead, anyone can practise Wicca either as their sole religion, or – a popular choice – alongside another faith. Freedom of religion is legally protected in the UK, and Paganism (an umbrella term under which witchcraft falls) is recognized as a valid faith. But also, many witches have shaken off the Gardnerian idea of witchcraft as a religion.

As we have discovered during the course of this book, the history of magic and witchcraft is both long and colourful. It is a thread that has always been woven through human experience, and because it speaks to the needs of the heart, there is no sign that it will ever run out.

The pendulum is swinging away from the virtual world of the web, with increasing numbers of practitioners revaluing the direct experience of withcraft and magic.

Mu Revealed *by Tony Earll (nom de plume of Raymond Buckland) which describes a successful archeological expedition to find the manuscript of a priest of Mu.*

Modern witches prefer real life rituals to virtual ones, ensuring that magic in real life continues to this day.

Select Bibliography

Apollonius of Rhodes, trans. Rieu, E.V. *The Voyage of Argo*. (Harmondsworth: Penguin, 1976)

Apuleius, trans. Graves, Robert. *The Golden Ass*. (Harmondsworth: Penguin, 1972)

Baker, Jim. *The Cunning Man's Handbook*. (London: Avalonia, 2013)

Barnes, Jonathan, trans. *Early Greek Philosophy*. (Harmondsworth: Penguin, 1987)

Betz, Hans Dieter, trans. and ed. *The Greek Magical Papyri in Translation*. (Chicago and London: University of Chicago Press, 1996)

Branston, Brian. *The Lost Gods of England*. (London: Thames and Hudson, 1984)

Callow, John. *Embracing the Darkness: A Cultural History of Witchcraft*. (London: IB Tauris, 2018)

Churton, Tobias. *The Magus of Freemasonry*. (Rochester, VT: Inner Traditions, 2006)

Cochrane, Robert, with Jones, Evan John. *The Robert Cochrane Letters*. (Milverton, Somerset: Capall Bann, 2002)

French, Peter. *John Dee*. (London: Ark, 1987)

Gosden, Chris. *The History of Magic: From Alchemy to Witchcraft, From the Ice Age to the Present*. (London: Penguin/Viking, 2020)

Gardner, Gerald. *The Meaning of Witchcraft*. (Wellingborough, Northants. Aquarian Press, 1959)

Graves, Robert. *The White Goddess*. (London: Faber and Faber, 1961)

Griffiths, Bill. *Aspects of Anglo-Saxon Magic*. (Hockwold-cum-Wilton: Anglo-Saxon Books, 1996)

Heselton, Philip. *Doreen Valiente: Witch*. (Doreen Valiente Foundation with The Centre for Pagan Studies, 2016)

In Search of the New Forest Coven. (Nottingham: Fenix Flames, 2020.)

Homer, trans. Rieu, E.V. *The Odyssey*. (Harmondsworth: Penguin, 1969)

Howe, Katherine, ed. *The Penguin Book of Witches*. (New York: Penguin, 2014)

Hutton, Ronald. *Stations of the Sun*. (Oxford: Oxford University Press, 1996)

The Triumph of the Moon. (Oxford: Oxford University Press, 1999)

The Witch. (New Haven and London: Yale University Press, 2018)

Iamblichus, trans. Clarke, Emma C., Dillon, John M and Herschbell, Jackson P. *On the Mysteries.* (Atlanta, GA: Society of Biblical Literature, 2003

Jones, Evan John and Cochrane, Robert. *The Roebuck in the Thicket.* (Milverton, Somerset: Capall Bann, 2001.

Josten, C.H., ed. *Elias Ashmole.* (Oxford: Clarendon Press, 1966, five volumes)

Kerenyi C. *The Gods of the Greeks.* (London: Thames and Hudson, 1982)

Leland, Charles Godfrey. *Aradia, Or the Gospel of the Witches.* Dumfries & Galloway: Anodos, 2018.

Liddell, William. *The Pickingill Papers.* (Milverton: Capall Bann, 1994.

Luck, Georg, trans. *Arcana Mundi.* (Baltimore: Johns Hopkins University Press, 2006)

Malory, Sir Thomas. *Le Morte d'Arthur.* (London: Dent, 1967, two volumes)

Marinus of Samaria, trans. Guthrie, Kenneth S. *The Life of Proclus.* (Grand Rapids, MI: Phanes Press, 1986)

Parry, Glyn. *The Arch-Conjuror of England: John Dee.* (New Haven and London: Yale University Press, 2011)

Plotinus, trans. MacKenna, Stephen. *The Enneads.* (London: Penguin, 1991)

Poole, Robert, ed. *The Wonderful Discovery of Witches in the County of Lancaster by Thomas Potts.* (Lancaster: Palatine, 2011)

Proclus, trans. Ronan, S. *On the Sacred Art.* (Hastings: Cthonius Books, 1989)

Robbins, Rossell Hope. *The Encyclopaedia of Witchcraft and Demonology.* (Girard and Stewart, 2015)

Ross, Anne. *The Pagan Celts.* (Ruthin; John Jones Publishing Ltd., 1998)

Russell, Jeffrey B. and Alexander, Brooks. *A New History of Witchcraft.* (London: Thames and Hudson, 2018)

Thomas, Keith. *Religion and the Decline of Magic.* (London: Weidenfeld & Nicholson, 1997)

Valiente, Doreen. *Natural Magic.* (London: Robert Hale, 2016)

The Rebirth of Witchcraft. (London: Robert Hale, 2016)

Witchcraft for Tomorrow. (London: Robert Hale, 2012)

Waldron, RA, ed. *Sir Gawain and the Green Knight.* (London: Edward Arnold, 1971)

Walker, D.P. *Spiritual and Demonic Magic from Ficino to Campanella.* (Stroud: Sutton Pubs., 2000)

Wilby, Emma. *The Visions of Isobel Gowdie.* (Brighton: Sussex Academic Press, 2013)

Yates, Frances A. *The Rosicrucian Enlightenment.* (London: Ark, 1986

Index

Picture Credits

Acknowledgements

I owe a profound debt of gratitude to all the historians who have, over recent decades, revolutionised the study of witchcraft and folk magic. Foremost amongst these must stand Ronald Hutton, but I am also particularly indebted to the work of Emma Wilby and Owen Davies. Any errors in the text are, of course, my own.

Christina Oakley Harrington has established Treadwell's Bookshop in London as an invaluable hub of learning about esoteric subjects. Many thanks to her and all the wonderful staff for research materials and for many a happy hour spent both giving and listening to lectures.

My brilliant editor Tania O'Donnell has combined her skills and talent with unfailing good humour; working with her has been a true pleasure.

And lastly, my husband Patric has listened to my babblings about witchcraft and magic with exceedingly good grace. I hereby promise never to turn him into a frog.